The Olmec and Toltec: The History of Early Mesoamerican Cultures

By Charles River Editors

A sculpted head made by the Olmec circa 1200-900 B.C. Photo by Maribel Ponce Ixba

About Charles River Editors

Charles River Editors is a boutique digital publishing company, specializing in bringing history back to life with educational and engaging books on a wide range of topics. Keep up to date with our new and free offerings with this 5 second sign up on our weekly mailing list, and visit Our Kindle Author Page to see other recently published Kindle titles.

We make these books for you and always want to know our readers' opinions, so we encourage you to leave reviews and look forward to publishing new and exciting titles each week

Introduction

The Olmec

An Olmec mask made of jade.

    The Olmec people are widely recognized as the first major civilization of Mexico and are thus generally regarded as the mother civilization of Mesoamerica, making them the people from which all subsequent Mesoamerican cultures derived. In fact, the term Olmec is thought to have originated with the Aztec people, as Olmec in their Nahuatl language means "the rubber people", a reference to the inhabitants of the land from which they accessed rubber. By and large, the Olmec culture is perhaps best identifiable by their so-called colossal heads, mammoth basalt head-statues wearing helmet-like headdresses found throughout Olmec habitation sites.

    Around 2500 B.C., the Olmec settled primarily along Mexico's Gulf Coast in the tropical lowlands of south-central Mexico (in the modern-day States of Veracruz and Tabasco), and they flourished during North America's Prehistoric Indian Formative period from about 1700-400 B.C. Their direct cultural contributions were still evident as late as 300 A.D. Among Mesoamerican scholars, the Formative period is subdivided into the Preclassic (Olmec period), Classic (Maya period), and Postclassic (Toltec and Aztec periods).

    The Olmec's agricultural abilities sustained them and ensured their power and influence for over a millennium. They produced corn/maize, squash, and other plant foods in such quantities that they were afforded the manpower to build great monuments and ceremonial centers to further promote their cultural identity. From a cultural standpoint, their pyramids, open plazas, their ballgame, and possibly even centers of human sacrifice are thought to have established the societal model that subsequent societies like the Maya, Zapotec, Teotihuacano, Toltec, Mixtec, and Aztec would emulate. In the same vein, some scholars believe that they also affected the cultural development of the Native American groups of the United States and those of Central and South America as well. Proving to be one the most enduring models ever, the religious and cultural structure the Olmec established held reign for over 3,000 years, and it would likely have endured much longer without the arrival of the Spanish conquistadors.

The Toltec

Toltec pyramid at Tula

Depiction of a snake-bird god, possibly Quetzalcoatl, at the Temple of Tlahuizcalpantecuhtli in Tula. Photo by HJPD

The Toltec are one of the most famous Mesoamerican groups in South America, but they are also the most controversial and mysterious. The Toltec have been identified as the group that established a strong state centered in Tula (in present-day Mexico), and the Aztec claimed the Toltec as their cultural predecessors, so much so that the word Toltec comes from the Aztec's word Tōltēcatl, translated as artisan. The Aztec also kept track of the Toltec's history, including keeping a list of important rulers and events, that suggest the peak of the Toltec occurred from about 900-1100 A.D.

From the moment Spanish conquistador Hernan Cortes first found and confronted them, the Aztecs have fascinated the world, and they continue to hold a unique place both culturally and in pop culture. Nearly 500 years after the Spanish conquered their mighty empire, the Aztecs are often remembered today for their major capital, Tenochtitlan, as well as being fierce conquerors of the Valley of Mexico who often engaged in human sacrifice rituals. Ironically, and unlike the Mayans, the Aztecs are not widely viewed or remembered with nuance, in part because their own leader burned extant Aztec writings and rewrote a mythologized history explaining his empire's dominance less than a century before the Spanish arrived.

Thus, even as historians have had to rely on Aztec accounts to trace the history and culture of the Toltec, they have had to deal with the fact that the evidence is fragmentary and incomplete. Given the fact that the Aztec leaders engaged in revisionist history, it becomes even more difficult to be sure that the Aztec accounts of the Toltec are accurate, with some scholars going so far as to call the Toltec culture nothing but myth.

While scholars continue to debate whether the Toltec were an actual historical group, there is an added layer of mystery to the fact that the settlement at Tula has a lot in common with the famous Mayan settlement at Chichén Itzá. The architecture and art at both sites are so similar that archaeologists and anthropologists have assumed they had the same cultural influences, even as historians struggle to determine the historical timelines, and thus whether Tula influenced Chichén Itzá or vice versa.

The Olmec and Toltec: The History of Early Mesoamerica's Most Influential Cultures comprehensively covers the history, culture, and lingering mysteries behind the Olmec and Toltec. Along with pictures depicting important people, places, and events, you will learn about the two groups like you never have before.

The Olmec and Toltec: The History of Early Mesoamerica's Most Influential Cultures

About Charles River Editors

Introduction

Olmec

Introductory Note

Chapter 1: The Origins of the Olmec

Chapter 2: The Rise of the Olmec Power Centers

Chapter 3: The Olmec Archeological Picture

Chapter 4: Olmec Religious Practices

Chapter 5: Olmec Mythology

Chapter 6: The Mesoamerican Ballgame

Chapter 7: Olmec Heritage

Toltec

Chapter 1: Mesoamerica

Chapter 2: Determining the Toltec Identity

Chapter 3: The Aztec Chronicles

Chapter 4: The Toltec Historical Picture

Chapter 5: The Toltec Religion

Chapter 6: Tollán

Chapter 7: The Toltec and Sorcery

Chapter 8: The Toltec's Legacy

Online Resources

Bibliography

Free Books by Charles River Editors

Discounted Books by Charles River Editors

Olmec

Introductory Note

Spelling of proper names of individuals, various Mesoamerican groups, and geographic locations can vary due to historical, cultural, and linguistic tradition. In this text, application of the singular Olmec rather than Olmecs is used according to scholarly, anthropological criteria, notwithstanding the fact that several scholars use the plural.

While the terms tribe and Indian are widely considered socially insensitive and historically inaccurate, they are used here in deference to traditional Mesoamerican history. Similarly, while the term civilization is considered subjective and Eurocentric, it is generally preferred by scholars of Central and South America and should be considered equivalent to the term culture.

Lastly, any inconsistencies regarding dates or sequence of events is a result of conflicting and often competing historical accounts.

Chapter 1: The Origins of the Olmec

Olmec painting in the Juxtlahuaca cave. Photo by Matt Lachniet, University of Nevada at Las Vegas

Mesoamerica is the name given to the geographical and cultural area in Central and North America generally encompassing the area from the desert north of the Valley of Mexico across Guatemala and Honduras (including Belize and El Salvador) to western Nicaragua and Costa Rica. It was in this region that a number of societies flourished before the Spanish conquest effectively ended the advancement of Mesoamerican cultures like the Aztec and India.

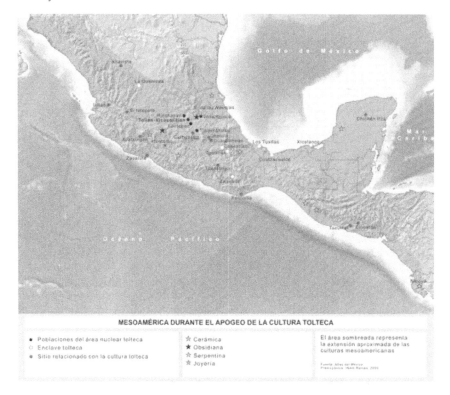

Map of Mesoamerican sites

As a cultural area, Mesoamerica is defined by the advent of a number of cultural traits developed and subsequently shared by indigenous populations of the region, beginning around 7000 B.C. with the farming of maize/corn, beans, squash, and chilis, as well as the domestication of turkeys and dogs. This subsequently set in motion a transition from migratory Paleoindian hunter-gatherer societies into organized, sedentary agricultural societies. Today, the groups are defined by their agricultural practices, distinct architectural styles, complex mythological and religious traditions, a calendar system, and a tradition of ball-playing.

The cultural evolution that took place in Mesoamerica prior to the arrival of Europeans is considered extraordinary by any measure. With evidence of potterymaking appearing in the fossil record by 2000 B.C., it seems science and technology clearly became motivational factors for the Olmec and subsequent cultures, if only to produce artifacts that were spiritual in significance. Art, for example, quickly evolved from simple referential imagery to symbolic writing, with texts varying in form and complexity based on the time period, the specific culture, and language. No true alphabet was ever developed for these early forms of writing, making decipherment arduous even for modern linguists.

Other art involved not just the graphic (used to express ideological concepts or features of nature) but the monumental, such as the advent of flat-topped pyramids thought by many historians to have spawned the "moundbuilder" traditions in North America, as exemplified by the Adena and Hopewell of Ohio, and the Mississippian of the Mississippi River Valley and U.S. Southeast. Scholars do not know with certainty which cultures conceived and developed various other innovations, but metalworking, astronomy, arithmetic, the calendar, and advanced irrigation techniques are typically attributed to the Mesoamerican people. The overlapping of Maya, Teotihuacano, Toltec, and Aztec histories makes it nearly impossible to discern who to credit with these and other advances, but given all of these cultural advancements, it stands to reason that one of the most influential civilizations in the region is the oldest.

By all indications, once the settlement process began, within just a few centuries, a major independent culture emerged from the lowlands of Veracruz and Tabasco on the Gulf Coast of Mexico: the Olmec. One of the earliest known complex civilizations of Mesoamerica, the Olmec settled the Gulf Coast of Mexico and then extended its sphere of influence inland and southwards across the Isthmus of Tehuantepec. This period of cultural development also saw the institution of class stratification, an establishment of chiefdoms with large corresponding ceremonial centers, and the organization of a network of interconnected trade routes for dealing cacao, ceramics, cinnabar, hematite, jade, obsidian, and Spondylus shells.

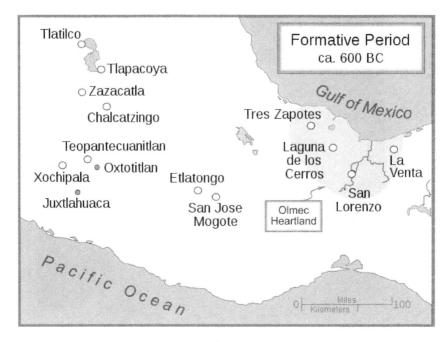

A map of the region

Although interest in Mesoamerican civilizations had picked up by the late 19th century, the existence of the Olmec civilization was only first ascertained through examination of artifacts acquired by antiquity dealers purchased via the pre-Columbian art market in the late 19th and early 20th centuries. While all Olmec artwork is striking in style and execution, as exemplified by exquisite representations of jaguar crafted from jade, it is the giant colossal basalt head statues - some weighing more than 20 tons - that have provided the greatest insight into the Olmec culture. With discovery of the first such giant head in 1862 near the Veracruz district of San Andres Tuxtla, scholars were able to get a clue about the Olmec sphere of influence, because basalt (a type of volcanic rock) is not indigenous to the Gulf Coast region and thus had to have been transported great distances over land and water to accommodate their sculpting needs.

One of the Olmec's colossal heads

Statue depicting a were-jaguar (baby jaguar)

When archaeologists first began excavation of the Olmec heartland, an area now demarcated as lying between the Tuxtla Mountains and the Olmec principal site of La Venta and extending some 50 miles inland from the Gulf of Mexico, they began to discover Olmec artifacts far from the Gulf Coast. Given the distance, they were initially doubtful the ancient inhabitants were actually Olmec, figuring instead that they were finding remains from other Mesoamerican groups who had acquired Olmec objects through trade. Ultimately, the realization that the Olmec had successfully established and maintained far-flung trade to acquire basalt, jade, magnetite, and serpentine ore provided the first significant insight into the workings of Olmec society.

Though far from clearly defined even today, it is apparent that the Olmec religious system influenced all successive Mesoamerican cultures, including the Maya, Zapotec, Teotihuacano,

Toltec, Mixtec, and Aztec, up to and even beyond the arrival of the Spanish in 1519. But their contribution to complex societal development in Mesoamerica and even the whole of Mexico is far more significant. While is has been argued that the Olmec were not the first organized culture in the area, evidence suggests that their settlement at San Lorenzo most likely represents the first major population center. San Lorenzo was the first city to be founded with a ceremonial center/pyramid-mound at its core (a center requiring the moving of millions of cubic tons of earth by the basketload), the first socially-organized, advanced metropolis (with a stratified society segregated into priest, merchant, and craftsmen classes), the first fully-actualized commerce center (where Mesoamerican traders dealt in exotic goods including salt, cocoa beans, bird feathers, jaguar pelts, and grinding stones), and monumental art reflecting hero-gods or perhaps ruler lineage.

Considering the time that has passed since the peak of the Olmec, it is impossible to know with certainty the actual linguistic roots of the Olmec people, but that has not stopped linguists from speculating about their language. Among the most widely considered is that offered by University of Hawaii professor of linguistics Lyle R. Campbell and University of Pittsburgh professor of anthropology Terrence Kaufman. In 1976, they published a paper in which they proposed that the presence of a number of core loanwords (common words adopted cross-lingually that are largely resistant to linguistic evolution) had apparently spread from a Mixe–Zoquean language into many other Mesoamerican languages. The Mixe–Zoquean language family is thought indigenous to the area around the Isthmus of Tehuantepec, Mexico, and it is also related to the Maya language family. Campbell and Kaufman suggested that the presence of these loanwords indicate that the Olmec spoke a language ancestral to Mixe–Zoquean.

This theory was challenged by a Danish Mixe–Zoque language specialist, Søren Wichmann, who instead argued that the Mixe–Zoquean loanwords appear to have originated in the Zoquean branch of the lingual family (a branch indigenous to southern Mexico). Wichmann argued that this indicated the loanword transmission occurred in the period after the two branches of the language family split, thus placing the time of the borrowings outside the Olmec era. However, in more recent years, new evidence has surfaced that indicates the proposed date of the split of the Mixean and Zoquean languages should be pushed back, which would place it well within the Olmec era. Subsequently, Wichmann himself modified his perspective, subsequently suggesting that the Olmec of San Lorenzo Tenochtitlán spoke protoMixe, while the Olmec of La Venta spoke protoZoque.

Regardless, since the Mixe–Zoquean languages have for centuries been historically associated with the area corresponding to what is recognized as the Olmec heartland, most scholars assume the Olmec spoke one or more Mixe–Zoquean languages/dialects, and may have varied site to site.

Chapter 2: The Rise of the Olmec Power Centers

By the latter half of the 20th century, it became evident that the core of the Olmec culture lay in the area of the Papaloapan, Coatzacoal, and Tonala rivers in what is now Central Mexico. In the early Formative period, from about 1500-900 B.C., urban areas with many specialized buildings and a stratified society emerged from what had previously been a sedentary agricultural and artisan society. According to Mesoamericanist scholars, shaman-kings emerged from the Olmec elite class, and they subsequently gained political dominance by providing a spiritual and cultural framework for creation and the cycles of human life by interpreting signs they believed were provided by the cosmos. To further dramatize the king's power, elaborate ceremonial sites were then established under regional chiefs, who organized state labor forces that further engrained the king's authority.

The first settlement to become the focal point of this increasingly intensified Olmec kingly power was San Lorenzo. Centered along the Gulf of Mexico's Bay of Campeche in the tropical lowlands of south-central Mexico, the Olmec erected permanent city-temple complexes at San Lorenzo that by some definition might be considered their own city-states. These complexes actually consisted of three related archaeological sites at San Lorenzo, Tenochtitlán, and Potrero Nuevo, but San Lorenzo Tenochtitlán (not to be confused with the Aztec capital of Tenochtitlan in Mexico City) is the collective name for the settlement. Serving as a major Olmec center from approximately 1200-900 B.C., and by far the largest city in Mesoamerica at this time, San Lorenzo is best known today for the many colossal stone basalt heads unearthed there. 10 have already been found, and the largest weighs more than 20 tons and stood nearly 10 feet tall. Perhaps not surprisingly, upon seeing the giant heads, several early archaeologists immediately associated them with the famed Moai on Easter Island, the monolithic human figures carved from rock by the indigenous Rapa Nui people between 1250-1500 A.D.

Locations of the major Olmec settlements of San Lorenzo Tenochtitlán, La Venta, Tres Zapotes, and Laguna de los Cerros

Frontal and side photo of a colossal head found at San Lorenzo Tenochtitlán

Rising in the midst of a large and lush agricultural area, San Lorenzo was built around a ceremonial center, perhaps the first flat-top pyramid in Mesoamerica, and it is thought to have supported a medium-to-large agricultural population, with housing suggesting nearly 6,000 residents within the settlement and upwards of 13,000 when including the outlying habitation sites. The settlement, which had no walls, covered over 1700 acres, and San Lorenzo proper covered 135 acres that were significantly modified through extensive filling and leveling. By one estimate, 500,000-2 million cubic meters of earth were moved by the basketload to provide landfill.

Although the Olmec would ultimately establish four principal cultural centers, San Lorenzo holds incomparable historical significance because it is regarded by many historians as the birthplace of civilization in Mesoamerica, and by some reckoning, it may represent the first fully-defined city in the Western Hemisphere. San Lorenzo is thought to have reached its height of power and influence between 1200-900 B.C., and it may have sustained a population of 11,000-18,000 before the city was ultimately abandoned in favor of their new site at La Venta.

The establishment and rise of civilization at San Lorenzo was made possible by the well-watered alluvial soil (built up by successive layers of river silt), and the natural transportation network provided by the Coatzacoalcos River Basin. This is comparable to other ancient civilization centers, including Egyptian settlements along the Nile River, settlements along the Indus River in India, and Sumerian settlements near the Tigris and Euphrates Rivers in Mesopotamia. The region around San Lorenzo had enough natural resources to maintain a settlement that was unprecedented for the time, and Olmec builders utilized the resources that were at their disposal to come up with engineering feats like drainage systems constructed out of stone-carved pipes.

During the early stages of San Lorenzo's development, Olmec leaders recognized the value of nearby resources like basalt and quickly established a trade system with neighboring groups (perhaps early Maya) to acquire jade (traced to the Motagua River Valley in eastern Guatemala), obsidian (traced to sources in the Guatemala highlands), and magnetite (traced to various sources 120-250 miles away). The success of this trade system triggered the rise of an elite class within Olmec society, which led to a growing demand for symbolic and luxury items made out of exotic materials. These artifacts not only came to define Olmec culture but also made San Lorenzo a powerful regional center politically, and since it was one of the first Mesoamerican cities (if not the first), San Lorenzo did not have to contend with powerful rivals or compete for resources.

In spite of its dynamic beginnings, San Lorenzo fell into steep decline by 900 B.C., with the city abandoned for La Venta a few generations later, but limited occupation continued for centuries. Although climatic and environmental changes are linked to the demise of San Lorenzo, many historians suspect other factors were at play that might explain why later sculptures were carved out of earlier ones and others were only half-completed. This suggested to some that rival groups may have fought over control of the resources, but other researchers believe that diseases or other natural phenomena led to a reduction in San Lorenzo's population, which might have made it impossible to quarry and transport new stone. While scholars continue to debate the circumstances of San Lorenzo's decline, most contend that despite the seemingly dramatic events surrounding it, the transition to La Venta appears to have gone relatively smoothly, as if it was planned.

San Lorenzo is believed to have been a power center that dominated much of the Coatzacoalcos Basin for nearly three centuries, so it is not surprising that some of the best architectural and technological work of the era was achieved there. For example, archaeologists have suggested that as a highly-advanced living center, San Lorenzo city planners were able to supply this city of commerce with not only drinking water but water for ritual purposes via an elaborate drainage system using channeled stones as a type of underground pipeline. In fact, University of Illinois anthropologist Ann Cyphers has theorized that the city's rulership was intimately linked to a supernatural patron figure associated with water.[1]

However, archaeological evidence indicates that by 900 B.C., San Lorenzo began to be surpassed in importance by the settlement located at La Venta. By 800 B.C., San Lorenzo was

---

[1] *Cyphers, Ann. From Stone to Symbols: Olmec Art in Social Context at San Lorenzo Tenochtitlán. Page 165.*

apparently all but abandoned, despite evidence of significant recolonization efforts from 600-400 B.C. and again from 800-1000 A.D. After the first major Olmec settlement began to wane, La Venta, located in the present-day Mexican State of Tabasco, began to take on more importance, and it had eventually risen to prominence by 1000 B.C. Scholars have offered a number of explanations for this shift in geographic focus, and the destruction of many of San Lorenzo's monuments around 950 B.C. has led some to suspect civil war or outside invasion, but given the lack of walls, most scholars believe that San Lorenzo was a relatively peaceful place that didn't face a threat of war. Most Mesoamerican scholars believe environmental changes necessitated the move, perhaps once certain important rivers changed course. The notion that there was a conflict is also refuted by the existing evidence, which suggests an orderly and methodical transition took place from one center to the other.

La Venta was designed as a fully-functional civic and ceremonial center, and it was apparently of a higher order than San Lorenzo, since it included spectacular visual displays of power and wealth not present at San Lorenzo. Located on an island in a coastal swamp overlooking the then-active Río Palma, La Venta's sphere of influence probably extended across the region between the Mezcalapa and Coatzacoalcos rivers. The site itself is nearly 10 miles inland, with the island consisting of slightly more than two square miles of dry land resting on the largest alluvial plain in Mexico (a flat landform created by the deposit of sediment over a long period of time).

While royal residences have yet to be identified or excavated, it appears that the non-royal elite and commoners of La Venta actually resided on the periphery of the city in outlying sites such as San Andrés, located about three miles northeast of La Venta proper in the Grijalva River Delta area of the Tabasco Coastal Plain. Thus, instead of providing residential areas, La Venta was dominated by a restricted sacred area that archaeologists refer to as Complex A, a mound and plaza group located just to the north of the Great Pyramid and thought to have been restricted to the Olmec elite class. The northern orientation of Complex A also happens to align it with the North Star, suggesting the Olmec were at least passingly familiar with some astronomical observations.

La Venta also has Complex C, which consists of the Great Pyramid and the large associated plaza to the south. South of the Great Pyramid lies Complex B, a 440-yard by 110-yard plaza that appears to have been built specifically for large public gatherings, with a layout suggesting that the surrounding platforms functioned as stages where ritual dramas were performed for the population at large.

Remnants of Complex A

The grand pyramid located at La Venta

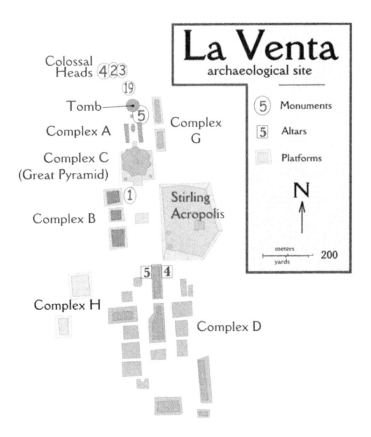

Archaeological layout of the settlement at La Venta

The layout of La Venta suggests its primary purpose was as a ceremonial center, replete with tombs, stone monuments, stelae, and what are thought to be altars all painstakingly arranged among the mounds and platforms. All of this suggests worship and/or forms of veneration may have taken place at countless locations around the city, though the platforms' wooden structures, including sanctuaries or observatories or even charnel houses (structures filled with bones and then ceremonially burned), have long since disappeared. Buried deep within La Venta, archaeologists have uncovered opulent, labor-intensive offerings, including 1,000 tons of smooth serpentine block, large mosaic pavements, and at least 48 separate deposits of polished jade celts, pottery, figurines, and hematite mirrors. All of this indicates the level of social and economic power and influence the city commanded at its peak. By most estimates, La Venta was fully occupied from approximately 900-400 B.C., and it would have required a population of at least 18,000 to maintain itself during its principal occupation.

An Olmec tomb at La Venta.

This buried mosaic unearthed at La Venta includes hundreds of serpentine blocks. Photo by Rubin Charles

An altar found at La Venta. Photo by Rubin Charles

This monument, found in Complex A at La Venta, is the earliest known depiction of a feathered serpent, a common motif among subsequent Mesoamerican groups. Photo by Audrey and George Delange

Located in the south-central Gulf Lowlands of Mexico in the Papaloapan River Plain, Tres Zapotes is usually considered the third successive Olmec capital or principal city after San Lorenzo Tenochtitlán and La Venta, but as a cultural center, it is considered atypical in form and function when compared to earlier Olmec sites or subsequent Mesoamerican cities. Founded sometime around 1200-1000 B.C., Tres Zapotes emerged as a regional center early in the Middle Formative period, perhaps around 900 B.C., which generally corresponds with the decline of San Lorenzo. That said, the earliest public architecture thus far discovered at this site has been dated to the end of the Middle Formative, perhaps 500 B.C.

Erected at what is essentially a transition point between the Los Tuxtlas Mountains and the Papaloapan River Delta, the location allowed the residents to take advantage of the forested highlands, as well as the swamps and streams of the flatlands. Additionally, scholars have speculated that choosing this location may have been motivated by the close proximity to Cerro El Vigía, an extinct volcano just six miles to the east that provided basalt, which was required for the production of their distinctive colossal heads. The volcano also provided other stones, as well as sandstone and clay. In fact, scholars have found evidence that suggests the nearby small site of Rancho la Cobaa, located on the northern flank of Cerro El Vigía, may have functioned as a monument-producing factory. Most of the basalt stonework at Tres Zapotes were crafted from the giant smooth-faced boulders found even today at the summit of Cerro El Vigía.

To date, over 160 mounds, platforms, and similar structures have been uncovered at Tres Zapotes, which archaeologists have concluded were built mostly for residential purposes. The mound locations and public architecture are positioned in ways that suggest a growing tendency towards decentralized political structure, as opposed to La Venta's architecture, which reflected a heavily centralized rulership. It has been theorized that each mound group was indicative of a different segment of society in the settlement, a trend that would gradually grow all the way to the Epi-Olmec (Post-Olmec) period. For example, at La Venta, three of the four colossal heads were grouped together at the front of a ceremonial area, while the fourth was positioned at the edge of the large central plaza. Conversely, the two excavated heads at Tres Zapotes were not in the central group.

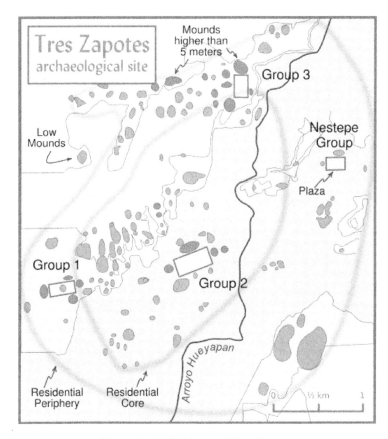

The archaeological layout of Tres Zapotes

The layout of Tres Zapotes' four mound groups is similar to the groups found at Cerro de Las Mesas, and together, the two settlements are believed to have constituted the center of the subsequent Epi-Olmec culture. The mound groups consisted of a large plaza surrounded by several mounds, with one mound shaped like a pyramid to the west and a longer mound to the north. Scholars have suggested that the longer mounds might have been the location of residences for elite classes or perhaps for administrative centers, while smaller mounds were for temples or other inhabitants' homes, because the different mounds are noticeably different in terms of size and complexity. Since the elite classes could afford more, it would make sense that their opulence helped pay for better sites.

Although construction activity continued at Tres Zapotes through the Classic Era (which began about 300 A.D.) and the settlement remained an important region for the Olmec, Tres Zapotes began losing its prestige to the Classic Veracruz culture, which was starting to grow more prominent at the time. It's widely assumed that as the Classic Veracruz continued to consolidate power, the Olmec grew steadily weaker from 600-1200 A.D. That said, Tres Zapotes did not disappear as quickly, like La Venta did at the close of the Middle Formative period, nor was it immediately affected by the deterioration of the Olmec's fortunes. In fact, it's believed that Tres Zapotes was not abandoned until as late as 900 A.D.

This vessel found at Tres Zapotes dates to around 300 B.C. – 250 A.D.

The fourth major Olmec habitation site, Laguna de Los Cerros, was located near Corral Nuevo in the southern foothills of the Tuxtla Mountains. Likely settled around 1400 B.C. and becoming a regional center covering as much as 370 acres by 1200 B.C., Laguna de Los Cerros (meaning "lake of the hills") was home to about 100 mounds and is believed to have been a pivotal point for traders between the Mexico Highlands and Tuxtepec trade routes, as it is located in a pass between the river valleys to the south and the northwest and was a crucial source of basalt cut from the volcanic Tuxtla Mountains to the north. While it is associated with the Olmec, archaeological evidence indicates that Laguna de Los Cerros was occupied over an uncharacteristically long period of time, perhaps as long as 2000 years.

Though recognized as a principal Olmec settlement, Laguna de Los Cerros has been the least investigated or studied of the four major Olmec centers, as it was only briefly surveyed by Alfonso Medellin Zenil in 1960 and by Dr. Ann Cyphers in the late 1990s and early 2000s. Fundamentally, the layout of the site features long parallel mounds with large rectangular plazas, with conical mounds demarcating plaza endpoints. Though the layout and mounds have similarities with those found at other Olmec settlements, most of the mounds date to the post-Olmec Classical era, roughly 250-900 A.D.

Furthermore, one of Laguna de Los Cerros' satellite sites was Llano del Jícaro, which seems to have been a monumental architecture workshop established near the basalt flows that produced stoneworks found not only at Laguna de Los Cerros but San Lorenzo Tenochtitlán some 37 miles to the southeast. Many historians assume that as a satellite of Laguna de Los Cerros, Llano del Jícaro was also effectively a satellite of San Lorenzo Tenochtitlán, either directly or through control of Laguna de Los Cerros (perhaps through chiefdom administration).

Llano del Jícaro appears to have been abandoned sometime after 1000 B.C., with Laguna de Los Cerros showing a significant, simultaneous decline. While the cause of this decline is unknown, since it occurred within the same timeframe as the decline and abandonment of San Lorenzo, most scholars believe it suffered the same fate as a result of the environmental impact of a severe shift in the course of the San Juan River.

Chapter 3: The Olmec Archeological Picture

Prior to the first significant findings of the mid-19th century, the Olmec culture was unknown to historians and largely believed to be figures of Aztec or Maya mythology. In 1869, however, Mexican explorer José Melgar y Serrano reported that a colossal head had been discovered by a farmer clearing trees from his hacienda in Hueyapan (in the Mexican State of Veracruz). That said, other sources cite findings at El Manatí, a sacrificial bog with artifacts dating to 1600 B.C., as providing earlier evidence of the Olmec, and the colossal head, today labeled Tres Zapotes Monument A, had actually been discovered in the late 1850s and left partially embedded until Melgar y Serrano visited the site in 1862 and exposed it With this discovery, American, European, and Mesoamerican historians were anxious to find out more about this mysterious culture and distinguish it from the more familiar Maya and Aztec, a task that is still ongoing.

Within just a few decades, a number of other Olmec artifacts such as the jade Kunz axe, an 11 jade head shaped like an axe but thought to have served a ritual rather than functional purpose, came to light and was subsequently recognized as part of the Olmec Tradition. In the 1920s, work began in the Tuxtla Mountains at La Venta and San Martin under the direction of anthropologists Frans Blom (1893-1963) and Oliver La Farge (1901-1963), at which time the San Martin Pajapan Monument 1 was re-discovered (after first identified by surveyor Ismael

Loya in 1897). Found on top of the San Martin Pajapan volcano, this 5'6 tall basalt sculpture was likely carved during the Early Formative period before 1000 B.C. and depicts a crouching young Olmec lord said to be caught in the act of raising a large ceremonial bar with his right hand under one end and his left over the other. In addition to the monument, researchers found all sorts of other religious offerings, including vessels and jade objects, and by dating the remains, they have speculated that the mountaintop has been considered a sacred site for over 2,000 years. At the time the monument and other objects were found, however, many archaeologists assumed the Olmec were actually contemporaries of the Maya, not predecessors. In fact, Blom and La Farge attempted to explain what they found by suggesting it was the Maya who had influenced the Olmec culture.[2]

---

[2] *Coe, Michael D.* America's First Civilization: Discovering the Olmec. *Page 40.*

Picture of the Kunz axe.

Picture of the San Martin Pajapan Monument 1

In the 1930s and 1940s, archaeologist Matthew Stirling (1896-1975) of the Smithsonian Institution conducted some of the first major excavations of the discovered Olmec sites, assisted in the endeavor by Mexican painter and ethnographer Miguel Covarrubias (1904-1957). During the course of this work, Stirling became convinced that the Olmec had actually flourished centuries before the other known Mesoamerican civilizations, but that assertion was challenged by contemporary archaeologists at the time, including J. Eric S. Thompson (1898-1975) and Sylvanus Morley (1883-1948) who dated the Olmec finds to the Classic era (200-1000 A.D.). The chronology issue was finally resolved in 1942 to most scholars' satisfaction at the Tuxtla Gutierrez Conference, during which noted Mexican archaeologist Alfonso Caso (1896-1970) conclusively persuaded the gathering that the Olmec were indeed the predecessors of other well-known Mesoamerican groups and had influenced them considerably. While subsequent advances in carbon-dating methods have reinforced Caso's contention, even today there are a number of scholars who remain unconvinced that the Olmec constitute the proto-Mesoamerican cultural group.

While Smithsonian archaeologist Mathew Stirling is often credited with identifying the Olmec civilization and fitting the Olmec culture into historical context, much of modern society's understanding of the Olmec is based on the fieldwork of Mayan scholar Michael D. Coe (1929-) due to his research at two principal Olmec sites: San Lorenzo Tenochtitlán and La Venta. With his well-established background in Mayan and other Mesoamerican cultures, he was able to provide a much-needed frame for all the work that preceded him.

San Lorenzo Tenochtitlán

After a cursory survey in 1938, the first significant excavation of the Olmec Heartland took place at San Lorenzo Tenochtitlán between 1946 and 1970 by archaeologist Matthew Stirling, who came up with the name San Lorenzo Tenochtitlán in 1955 and oversaw four archaeological projects at the site.

Following Stirling, Michael Coe visited San Lorenzo, determining that the site was first occupied soon after 1500 B.C., and that within the first century of settlement activity, the beginning of public works and architecture appeared (in the form of artificial mound build-up and raised platforms. Piecing together the larger sociocultural picture, Coe determined that the advent of earthworks at San Lorenzo were not unique to Mesoamerica but actually reflected a trend in ancient Mexico, where small villages coalesced to form larger labor forces specifically for the purposes of erecting structures of communal use. According to Coe, over the next few centuries, the major identifying Olmec cultural feature was the progress of the Olmec art-style, found both in artifacts and in the archaeological record, and by 1150 B.C. this style served to complement public architecture, complete with their unique jaguar iconography that may have depicted a deity in the form of a human-feline hybrid creature. Then, of course, there were the colossal basalt stone heads (found at San Lorenzo and other Olmec sites) that scholars believed were depictions of or tributes to early leaders. Coe further theorized "that the impetus for founding San Lorenzo was that the rich agricultural potential of the tropical environment and productive zones surrounding the large rivers could be exploited relatively easily without heavy investments of labor. The power that control of these rich lands would have offered to particular family groups or individuals might well have been symbolized and solidified by...relatively large-scale building and sculptural projects."[3]

---

[3] *Sabloff, Jeremy A.* The Cities of Ancient Mexico: Reconstructing a Lost World. *Page 41.*

A sculpture depicting a human-jaguar hybrid that was common in Olmec art.

La Venta

In 1940, archaeological attention was turned to the Olmec site of La Venta when Matthew Stirling and fellow archaeologist Philip Drucker (1911-1982) began detailed excavation funded by the National Geographic Society and the Smithsonian Institute. In 1943, Stirling and Drucker enlisted the help of archaeologist Waldo Rudolf Wedel (1908-1996), and the results were several articles published by Stirling and a two-volume monograph by Drucker in 1952. Drucker would also lead his own excavation in 1955, funded again by the National Geographic Society.

During a series of excavations, it was discovered that the arrangement of the mounds, platforms, complexes, and monumental artifacts at La Venta constituted four separate areas, subsequently designated Complexes A, B, C, and E, that in the words of Mesoamericanist Rebecca Gonzalez-Lauck "constitutes one of the earliest examples of large-scale ideological communications through the interaction of architecture and sculpture."4 Complex A, located just to the north of the Great Pyramid (Complex C), is thought to have been erected in four separate construction phases over a period of four centuries, roughly between 1000 B.C. and 600 B.C.. Surrounded by a series of basalt columns that may have been meant restrict access for only the elite class, three rectangular mosaics known as pavements were also unearthed at Complex A (each roughly 15x 20 feet and consisting of up to 485 blocks of serpentine), as well as five formal tombs, one with a sandstone sarcophagus carved with what appears to be a crocodilian-like monster.

The layout of Complex B has led scholars to assume it was built specifically for large public gatherings, unlike Complex A, which was seemingly reserved for the elite class. A plaza covering nearly 50,000 square yards with a small platform situated in the center, historians have proposed that the platforms surrounding the plaza may have functioned as stages where rituals were performed, and these rituals were likely associated with the monuments. What appear to be altars and stelae surrounding and within the plaza (including the now-famous Colossal Head 1/Monument 1) are positioned in such a manner so as to emote their meaning to many viewers simultaneously. Scholars frequently draw parallels between this staging arrangement and that of ancient Greek arenas.

Complex C, the Great Pyramid (one of the earliest pyramids known to Mesoamerica), is clearly the focal point of the entire city. Believed to have been built around the early 4th century B.C., the conical-shaped pyramid is 110 feet high and contains an estimated 100,000 cubic meters of earth fill. It had long been theorized that the pyramid was built to replicate nearby mountains, but recent work conducted by Mesoamericanist scholar Rebecca Gonzalez Lauck has shown that the pyramid was initially a rectangular pyramid with stepped sides and inset corners. It was only over the course of the last 2,500 years that it acquired its present shape, most likely due to wind erosion. As of June 2013, the Great Pyramid itself has never been excavated, leading anthropologists to continue to formulate theories as to its ultimate purpose.

Although there are no physical structures remaining in Complex E, it is widely believed to have once been a residential housing zone.

Tres Zapotes

Comparatively little archaeological work has been conducted at Tres Zapotes, but it was near this Olmec site that the first colossal head was discovered in 1862 by José Melgar y Serrano, and to date, two such heads have been found locally (labeled Monument A and Monument Q).

---

[4] *Gonzalez-Lauck, Rebecca. Venta, La (Tabasco, Mexico). Page 800.*

While most of the monumental sculptures found at Tres Zapotes date to the Late Formative period (the centuries just prior to 200 A.D.), well after the peak years of the Olmec, a number of revealing finds have been uncovered. For example, in 1939, archaeologist Matthew Stirling discovered the bottom half of Stela C, a slab of basalt with one side showing an Olmec-style engraving (depicting an abstract man-jaguar, or perhaps a ruler on a throne), while the other side displays the earliest Mesoamerican Long Count Calendar date yet unearthed, 7.16.6.16.18. Using a modern calendar, that date corresponds to September 3, 32 B.C. While the origin of this calendar system is unknown, the Long Count is commonly considered the Maya linear count of days, but in actuality, however, it is one of multiple interconnected cycles (though its extraordinary length of at least 5126 years makes it essentially a linear count through all of Mayan history.) Although there was some initial controversy over the missing first digit of Stela C, the issue was ultimately resolved in 1969 when the top half of the stela was located and the date was verified.

A chemical analysis of Stela C in 1965 concluded that unlike most other basalt stonework found at Tres Zapotes, that used for this stela is similar in composition to that used at La Venta for Stela 3 and the basalt columns surrounding La Venta Complex A, which have been traced to Punta Roca Partida on the Gulf Coast at the northern side of the Los Tuxtlas Mountains. For that reason, the making of the stela at Tres Zapotes is unusual and still somewhat mysterious, even as its association with the Olmec seems to be conclusively proven.

Superficially, Tres Zapotes has four mound groups similar in design to those at Cerro de Las Mesas, a site on the western edge of the Olmec heartland that rose to prominence after the decline of the Olmec culture.

Laguna de Los Cerros

Like Tres Zapotes, little excavation has taken place at Laguna de Los Cerros (only briefly investigated by Alfonso Medellin Zenil in 1960 and Dr. Ann Cyphers in the late 1990s and early 2000s), but surveys and fieldwork have provided valuable insight into the chronology of events at this once booming Olmec site. As one of four principal Olmec centers, Laguna de Los Cerros was likely settled between -1200 B.C., becoming a regional center whose primary objective was to oversee the Olmec monumental works conducted at the satellite site of Llano del Jícaro and to maintain control of the near-by basalt supply. Unlike the other three major Olmec centers, no colossal heads have been found at Laguna de Los Cerros, but roughly two dozen other Formative period monuments have been found, along with important samples of ceramic, basalt stone, and other materials that have helped scientists establish a sequence-of-events timeline.

Colossal Heads

By and large, the most recognized element of the Olmec culture are the 17 colossal basalt helmeted-heads distributed throughout most of their heartland. Since no known pre-Columbian text provides their history or purpose, these impressive monuments have been the subject of much scholarly speculation and debate. It was once theorized that the heads represent images of ancient Olmec ballplayers (representations of the helmet-wearing players associated with the game many believe to have been an Olmec invention), but they are now generally accepted as portraits of early rulers or perhaps famed hero-warriors. These rulers or hero-warriors may have been dressed as ballplayers or even perhaps in ritual attire that is still unfamiliar to modern scholars, but the most important aspect of the giant heads is that no two heads are alike, and their helmet-like headdresses are all unique as well. This has led scholars to believe they represented specific leaders, who may have been distinguished by their clan or class status. The 17 colossal heads found to date range in size from the pair found at Tres Zapotes (nearly 6 feet tall) to the Rancho La Cobata head (nearly 12 feet tall), with the largest weighing between 25 and 55 tons.

Interestingly, the colossal heads were carved from single blocks of volcanic basalt typically found miles away in the Tuxtlas Mountains. As chemical analysis has shown, the Tres Zapotes heads were sculpted from a variety of basalt found at the summit of Cerro El Vigía at the western end of the Tuxtlas, while the San Lorenzo and La Venta heads were likely carved from a variety found at Cerro Cintepec on the southeastern side and possibly manufactured at the nearby Llano del Jicaro workshop. The heads had to be dragged and/or floated to their final destination, leading some to speculate that it required as many as 1,500 workers three to four months to transport the heads to their final destination. As is evident today, some of the heads (like many of the monuments) experienced various forms of mutilation, disfigurement, burial, and relocation, with some monuments and at least two heads showing signs of being re-carved—but the motivation for these acts remains unclear. Scholars believe some forms of mutilation may have been part of a ritual, while others suggest it was a byproduct of internal conflict or civil uprisings. Others have suggested there might have been an outside invasion, but that seems less likely than the other explanations.

The African Origin Hypothesis

One of the more interesting and controversial theories regarding the famed colossal Olmec heads is that the flat-faced, thick-lipped features more closely resemble Africans than Mesoamericans, which some take as evidence of an African migration across the Atlantic. This hypothesis has been championed by a Guyanese-born Rutgers University Associate Professor of African Studies, Ivan van Sertima, who points out that the seven braids on the Tres Zapotes head was an Ethiopian hair style. However, most other Mesoamericanists reject the idea of any pre-Columbian contacts with Africa and attribute these features to the physical nature of the basalt material itself; based on the shallow space allowed on basalt boulders.

Additionally, scholars argue that even if the Olmec representations were intended to reflect actual, living individuals (which may or may not be the case), the broad noses, thick lips, and eyes bearing what is known as the Asian epicanthic fold (a prominent fold of skin on the upper eyelid said to have evolved to neutralize the effects of reflected sun) are all physical characteristics that can still be found in the modern Mesoamerican populations. Art historian Miguel Covarrubias (1904-1957) illustrated this fact in the 1940s with a series of photos of Olmec artwork that juxtaposed faces of modern Mexicans with very similar facial characteristics. Renowned American archaeologist and pre-Columbian Mesoamericanist scholar Richard Diehl also weighed in on this controversy in *The Olmecs: America's First Civilization*, writing, "There can be no doubt that the heads depict the American Indian physical type still seen on the streets of Soteapan, Acayucan, and other towns in the (Mesoamerican) region."[5]

Jade Masks

Another artifact that has garnered considerable attention and debate among Olmec scholars are a number of jade masks carved to resemble human faces. At the center of the controversy is the fact that these face masks have (to date) never been recovered from archaeologically-controlled Olmec sites, only from sites of other cultures, including one thought to have been deliberately deposited in the ceremonial district of Aztec Tenochtitlán. Dated to about 500 B.C., the mask in question would have been about 2,000 years old when the Aztec buried it, suggesting that such masks were highly valued or maybe even feared. Either way, not all Mesoamericanist scholars are convinced the masks are Olmec in origin, and similar masks were relatively common to the Hopewellian Moundbuilder sites in the United States.

---

[5] *Diehl, Richard A.* The Olmecs: America's First Civilization. *Page 112.*

A jade mask believed to have been an Olmec mask. Picture taken by Michael Wal.

Chapter 4: Olmec Religious Practices

While virtually nothing can be stated with certainty about the Olmec's spiritual beliefs, it is generally accepted that Olmec religious activities were performed by a combination of rulers, full-time priests, and perhaps shaman. Since their society was quite stratified, scholars believe that the Olmec rulers were considered the most important religious figures, and that they derived their legitimacy as rulers by associating themselves with Olmec deities.

According to oral tradition, the Olmec belief system (as well as those of subsequent Mesoamerican cultures) reflected a cosmic view in which all elements and creatures were infused with spiritual energy that provided the universe its momentum. Based on cross-cultural studies, particularly those of Native American societies, scholars speculate that the Olmec may have tried to gain access to this spiritual power through different kinds of disciplines and rituals, such as fasting, meditation, and possibly even physical mutilation and blood-letting. Some have gone so far as to assert that the Olmec routinely practiced violent forms of human sacrifice, such as decapitation, and then passed the practice on to other groups like the Maya.

Although their role is not clearly-defined, there is considerable physical evidence that the Olmec had shamans or some other form of holymen, particularly in the so-called transformation figures. Some historians have likened these shaman to astrologers, and there is some evidence that suggests shamans engaged in rituals designed to access animal spirits that could help transcend human consciousness. Olmec shamans may also have prepared special hallucinogens which were inhaled to induce altered states of consciousness, a ritual common to indigenous groups of both upper North America and South America. Olmec sculpture suggests that shaman attempted to assume the jaguar spirit using jade masks carved with a combination of feline and human features. As an animal whose existence combined the elements of land, water, and air through living in the jungle, swimming in rivers, lakes, and streams, and hunting both during the day and night, the jaguar clearly held special respect and spiritual significance. Olmec art and artifacts frequently depict jaguars, and the American eagle may have been perceived as the jaguar of the sky, with one sculpture portraying what has been interpreted as a flying jaguar with a human passenger on his back.

Chapter 5: Olmec Mythology

While no oral history about Olmec mythology survives, interpretations of monuments and other artifacts (such as the Las Limas figure at Veracruz), as well as studies of the mythology of subsequent Mesoamerican groups, have combined to offer a possible glimpse into what Olmec mythology may have been like. If accurate, it was a complex system of beliefs that were eventually replaced with legends about living Olmec hero-god rulers. Furthermore, Quetzalcoatl, the Feathered Serpent deity, is well represented in Olmec art, leading researchers to believe that the pantheon of deities found in Maya, Teotihuacano, Toltec, and Aztec culture can be traced all the way back to the Olmec.

The great bird-serpent/priest-king Quetzalcoatl is often compared to other ancient gods, like Ra for the ancient Egyptians, Enki for the Sumerians, and Nu Kua for the Chinese, but in Olmec culture, the Plumed Serpent was unique because he transformed from myth to god to human and back to myth, seemingly at will. Elusive and intangible, but at the same time permanent, the Olmec believed Quetzalcoatl would be physically incarnated at times, while at other times Quetzalcoatl essentially represented a kind of fairy tale story where anything is possible and things are constantly transforming into something else.

This Olmec artifact is the earliest known depiction of the serpent deity.

Conceived some 1500 years before the Biblical Christ, Quetzalcoatl not only formed the mythical basis for the Olmec religious worldview but was believed to have materialized as one or more living rulers, after which he went on to be held as a kind of religious messiah by numerous Mesoamerican cultures to follow. According to French anthropologist Claude Levi-Strauss, "all available variants of a myth must be taken into account. There is no single, true version"6, a perspective that can be aptly applied to the myth of Quetzalcoatl. Indeed, few mythological characters are deemed legends and afforded biographical status as Quetzalcoatl has.

---

[6] *Baldwin, Neil.* Legends of the Plumed Serpent: A Biography of a Mexican God. *Page 9.*

To the Aztec and several Mesoamerican cultures preceding them, history was not a straight linear timeline of events but a series of cycles described by Mexican historian Guillermo Batalla (1935-1991) as "a spinning wheel spiraling forward through time, engendering repetitions as it goes."7 According to Aztec beliefs, the god who set this wheel in motion was Plumed Serpent Quetzalcoatl, the Lord of the Dawn and Phoenix of the West. He was the namer of all things in the universe, and according to the Florentine Codex (the 16th century ethnographic account of Franciscan friar Bernardino de Sahagún), "He was the wind, he was the guide, the roadsweeper of the rain gods, of the masters of water, of those who brought rain. Legend recounts that Quetzalcoatl gathered together the remains of the human race from Mictlan (the Underworld; the Realm of the Dead) after the primeval flood and then reestablished humanity in the Time Before Time."

As the legend is told, Plumed Serpent took an assemblage of bones, ashes, and clay and infused his own sacred blood to form man, and then blessed him with maize, the arts of weaving and mosaic-making, music and dance, the science of curing illness, crafts, time, the stars in the heaven, the calendar, prayers, and sacrifice. Plumed Serpent was the performer of miracles, the supreme magician, the ruler of sorcerers, holding the secret of all enchantments.8 But as the legend further explains, Plumed Serpent's plans for humanity were frequently thwarted by his alter ego/dark side Tezcatlipoca, known also as Smoking Mirror, referred to in legend as his evil twin. Setting out to foil his good works, Tezcatlipoca posed as a servant to infiltrate Plumed Servant's holy monastery, then brewed pulque, a concoction derived from the maguey plant, which he served to Tezcatlipoca and his sister—then convinced him to have intercourse with her. Having broken his vows of chastity, Plumed Serpent was cast out of the monastery—scarred by his spiritual transgression. Now fallen from grace, Quetzalcoatl abandoned his earthly possessions and began what would become an epic hero's journey, beginning at Tollan (the future Toltec center).

Gaining fame throughout Mexico for his pilgrimage of purification, from Cholula (near present-day Puebla de Zaragoza in Central Mexico) to Chichen Itza, when Quetzalcoatl reached the shore of the holy sea at Tlillan Tlapallan (the Land of the Black and Red on the Gulf Coast of Mexico), he told his followers that he had been called forth, thus evolving into his messianic form. Directing his followers to build a raft of snakes, he donned a turquoise mask and promised to return in the year Ce Acatl or One Reed, a year that cycled every 52 years according to the calendar. Navigating out to sea, Plumed Serpent suddenly burst into flames, with the ashes of his heart rising upwards into the heavens and becoming the planet Venus. From that time on, he rose in the sky each morning to announce the rebirth of the sun.

Perhaps most notably, Ce Acatl corresponded to the year 1519 in the modern European calendar, which also happened to be the year Spanish ships first appeared on the horizon of

---

7 *Sahagun, Fray Bernardino de.* Florentine Codex.
8 *Baldwin, Neil.* Legends of the Plumed Serpent: A Biography of a Mexican God. *Pages 8—9.*

Veracruz. According to Aztec legend, the emperor, Montezuma, had stationed look-outs along the Gulf of Mexico in anticipation of Quetzalcoatl's fateful return and thus assumed Spanish conquistador Hernan Cortes was the Plumed Serpent returning as prophesied. Accordingly, the Aztec greeted Cortes with open arms and a mountain of gold; but within two years, the Aztec Empire fell to the Spanish. While that has long been the legend passed down orally, modern scholars believe the interactions between the Aztec and Spanish were considerably more nuanced and based on more geopolitical (and secular) matters.

Chapter 6: The Mesoamerican Ballgame

There is no single aspect of Mesoamerican culture with a greater range of speculation than the ballgame. Believed to have been a significant cultural feature throughout the societal development of Mesoamerica, perhaps dating back as far as 1600 B.C., it seems the ballgame was used for both recreational and religious purposes to varying degrees, and many scholars believe the Olmec are likely candidates for creators of this game. At the same time, while various scholarly sources have published detailed descriptions of the ballgame, no one in modern times can be certain of how the game was played, nor is it clear just how significant it was to society. That said, the modern Mesoamerican game of ulama, which is still played by indigenous populations in a few Central Mexico communities today, is thought to have derived from the original ballgame.

The largest ballgame court in Mesoamerica was at the Mayan city of Chichen Itza.

This carving in Veracruz depicts a ballplayer being sacrificed.

Judging by the varying elaborateness of the courts associated with the Maya, Toltec, Aztec, and a number of other related cultures of the region, scholars believe the game most likely carried varying significance among the different cultures. With rules differing according to cultural norms, the game may have been a death-sport involving human sacrifice in some societies (particularly the Maya), while in others, it may have simply been a recreational pastime played by children or even women.

To get a better understanding of the ballgame and the way the Olmec may have invented and played it, the best evidence comes from Mayan works and physical remains. In the game, two teams of 2-7 people moved a rubber ball by hitting it with the body without the use of hands or feet. The most effective method of directing the ball was through the use of the hips. The goal was to pass the ball through a vertical circular ring attached to the long wall of the court. The game was played on courts of various sizes and design, many with boundaries outlined by tall walls and shaped like the English capital letter "I." Protective gear shielded players from the impact of the heavy ball which varied in size from four to twelve inches in diameter and could weigh as much as seven pounds. A dozen rubber balls dated to 1600 B.C. have been found in El Manatí, an Olmec sacrificial bog about 6 miles east of San Lorenzo Tenochtitlán. Likewise, ballcourts varied considerably in size, from almost insignificant courts to highly impressive stadium-like settings. In each case, there were long, narrow alleys with walls along both sides, against which the balls could bounce.

Among the Mayans, the ballgame was played throughout all levels of society, from "sand lot" games to competitions with sacrificial consequences, occurring between the elites. Such games had grave consequences, and again depending on the variation, the losing team might be sacrificed to the gods. According to the *Popol Vuh*, two brothers, Hun Hunahpu and Vucub Hunahpu, were such skilled players and played so often that the noise of their games disturbed the lords of Xibalba (the Maya Underworld). The brothers were commanded to come to Xibalba to play a game, and guide owls were sent from Xibalba to guide the brothers to the underworld ball court. Hun Hunahpu and Vucub Hunahpu failed test after test from the death gods of Xibalba and were sacrificed the day after they arrived in the underworld. Hun Hunahpu's head was removed and mounted in a calabash tree as though in a *tzompantli* (skull rack), where the skulls of sacrificial victims were collected and displayed. The brothers' bodies were buried under the ball court.

This game or a variant of it was important in several Mesoamerican cultures, but based on the archeological evidence, the Maya considered it to be a central feature in their urban life. Sculpture associated with ball courts suggest that the game concluded with ritual human sacrifice, presumably captives, although some have suggested that the losing team or the captain of the team were treated to sacrificial execution. This procedure makes sense in the light of the theory that the game was a way of settling municipal grievances or inter-city wars. If the game was merely played for the sake of entertainment and competition, a ritual sacrifice of the losers would have been a rather severe method of improving the quality of play.

While there is no physical evidence to prove the Olmec used the ballgame as a bloodsport or associated the game with human sacrifice, many scholars believe an association developed between human sacrifice and the game within the span of the Classic era (200-1000 A.D.). Furthermore, researchers have found evidence suggesting ritual bloodletting in Olmec society, and depictions of human sacrifice can be found on the ballcourt panels of subsequent Mesoamerican settlements, including El Tajin (850-1100), Chichen Itza (900-1200), and on the well-known decapitated ballplayer stelae from the Classic Veracruz site of Aparicio (700-900)

Chapter 7: Olmec Heritage

Over 3,000 years after the Olmec rose to power, conference halls around the world continue to hold debates over the cultural influence of the Olmec, specifically whether they provided the social and cultural template for other Mesoamerican cultures or if they were merely a cultural parallel that flourished side by side with others. Although the traditional historical timeline places the Olmec first in a long succession of civilizations that culminated with the rise and fall of the Aztec Empire, there is a popular consensus among historians that it would be more accurate to consider the cultural developments from 1200 B.C.-1500 A.D. as one continuous complex system with a number of cultural variations across the region. Essentially, proponents of this perspective are asserting that the Olmec's economy, social structure, religion, ceremonial rituals, and trade innovations were so effective that there was little need for major adjustments in Mesoamerica over the course of nearly 3000 years. This perspective would make the Olmec culturally comparable to the Moundbuilder and Mississippian traditions that sprouted up across what is now the United States. Either way, the Olmec are recognized as the oldest known culture of Mesoamerica and are widely acknowledged as having an unparalleled effect on Mexico's cultural development.

Many people continue to be fascinated by Mesoamerican groups' lust for blood, whether through ritual bloodletting or actual human sacrifice, and all of this may have started with the Olmec, but it's still important to recognize the Olmec as a culture of firsts. Perhaps most importantly, the Olmec may have been the first people in the Western Hemisphere to develop a system of writing or at least a system of relating ideas and thoughts through iconography. During various excavations conducted as recently as 2002 and 2006, symbols found at San Andrés date back to 650 B.C., while speech scrolls and glyphs (similar to later Maya hieroglyphs) were dated back to 900 B.C. (predating the oldest known written language by at least 150 years). Furthermore, a writing tablet-sized serpentine slab dated to 1100-900 B.C. was found near San Lorenzo and contains a set of 62 complex symbols, 28 of which are unique and previously unknown to linguists. Adding to the intrigue is the fact that the serpentine slab bears little to no resemblance to any other Mesoamerican writing systems yet found.

Although it is the Mayan calendar that has fascinated modern society and conspiracy theorists, it's quite possible that the Long Count Calendar used by many Mesoamerican cultural groups may have been established by the Olmec. The Long Count Calendar was revolutionary because it used the number zero as a mathematical place-holder, and if it is Olmec in origin, this would represent one of the earliest uses of the zero concept in history. The concept that if no number appears in the place of tens in a calculation, then a "ṣifr" (Arabic for a small circle meaning empty) should be used to keep the rows straight and accurate is attributed to the Persian encyclopedist Muhammad ibn Ahmad al-Khwarizmi in the year 976 A.D. This circle eventually became the zero.

Proponents of this theory point to the fact that the artifacts reflecting the earliest Long Count Calendar dates were all discovered outside the immediate Maya homeland. In fact, three of the six artifacts were found within Olmec lands. However, others have countered that the Olmec civilization ended by the 4th century B.C., several centuries before the earliest yet-discovered artifact that represents a Long Count date, so linking the calendar all the way back to the Olmec remains tenuous.

<h3 style="text-align:center">Toltec</h3>

Chapter 1: Mesoamerica

The Toltec (TAHL tek) were a Nahuatl-speaking Mesoamerican warrior society of Chichimec stock that dominated a power-base centered near present-day Tula, Mexico, in the early Post-Classic period of Mesoamerican chronology (10th-12th centuries A.D). The Chichimeca designation today applies to a wide range of semi-nomadic, barbarian peoples who inhabited the area north of modern-day Mexico and the southwestern United States. The Nahuatl language, which has been spoken in Central Mexico since at least the 7th century A.D., is of the Nahuan branch of the Uto-Aztecan language family and is still spoken by an estimated 1.5 million Nahua people today. Nevertheless, it is most commonly associated with the Aztec Empire that dominated central Mexico during the Late Postclassic period of Mesoamerican history (14th-16th centuries A.D.).

Scholars still debate the origins of the name Toltec. Some believe that Toltec, which is said to mean "reed people", was derived from the original name of their capital city of Tollán, commonly translated as "place of rushes and reeds". According to other scholastic sources, Toltec also means people of Tula, as well as "urbanite" or "cultured person" in the Nahuatl language.

After gaining ascendancy in the Valley of Mexico by conquering the people of Teotihuacán (or by some accounts, simply waiting for their social/economic collapse), the Toltec founded Tollán near the modern town of Tula, about 50 miles north of Mexico City. While the full extent of their geographic influence is yet unknown, during a period of southward expansion beginning about 1000 A.D., it is widely believed they assumed control of the Maya of Yucatan from the 11th-13th centuries before their ultimate demise. This might explain the similarities between Tula and Chichén Itzá.

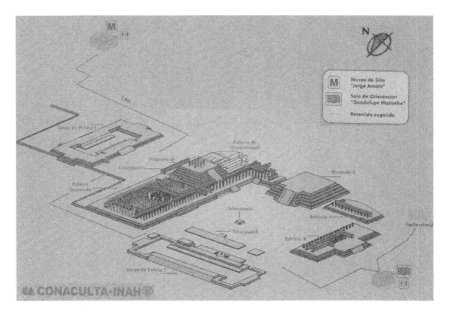

A computer generated layout of Tula based on archaeological work at the site. Photo by Susana Torres Sánchez

Mesoamerica is the name given to the geographical and cultural area in Central and North America generally encompassing the area from the desert north of the Valley of Mexico across Guatemala and Honduras (including Belize and El Salvador) to western Nicaragua and Costa Rica. It was in this region that a number of societies flourished before the Spanish conquest effectively ended the advancement of Mesoamerican cultures like the Aztec and India.

Map of Mesoamerican sites

As a cultural area, Mesoamerica is defined by the advent of a number of cultural traits developed and subsequently shared by indigenous populations of the region beginning around 7000 B.C. with the farming of maize/corn, beans, squash, and chilis, as well as the domestication of turkeys and dogs. This subsequently set in motion a transition from migratory Paleoindian hunter-gatherer societies into organized, sedentary agricultural societies. Today, the groups are defined by their agricultural practices, distinct architectural styles, complex mythological and religious traditions, a calendar system, and a tradition of ball-playing.

One of the earliest known complex civilizations of Mesoamerica was the Olmec culture (1700 B.C.- 400 B.C.), which settled the Gulf Coast of Mexico and then extended its sphere of influence inland and southwards across the Isthmus of Tehuantepec. This period of cultural development also saw the institution of class stratification, an establishment of chiefdoms with large corresponding ceremonial centers, and the organization of a network of interconnected trade routes for dealing cacao, ceramics, cinnabar, hematite, jade, obsidian, and Spondylus shells.

Chapter 2: Determining the Toltec Identity

While archaeological evidence has provided a great many clues about the Toltec culture, and the modern-day Pascua Yaqui have contributed considerable oral history to the Mesoamerican picture, most of what is known today about the Toltec comes from the so-called Aztec Chronicles, oral and written accounts that have faced decades of scrutiny from the world's top Mesoamerican scholars as they attempt to separate genuine history from historic distortions written to glorify Aztec rule.

After centuries of being categorized as an Aztec invention for the purpose of claiming a distinguished heritage, historians today identify the Toltec based on three other interrelated cultural groups: the Teotihuacanos (who are believed to have thrived as a society for nearly 750 years before the Toltec assumed control of their capital city of Teotihuacán and built Tollán on the ruins), the Aztec (who followed in the Toltec's footsteps and used their cultural model in founding their capital city of Tenochtitlan), and the Pascua Yaqui (a Uto-Azteca people said to have descended from the ancient Toltec and migrated into the United States by the end of 19th century.

According to the archaeological record, about 1 A.D., a culture known as the Teotihuacano emerged just outside modern-day Mexico City and began constructing a massive capital city that at its peak may have sustained a population of more than 200,000. Laid out in what would still be considered a modern design, Teotihuacán had wide streets, numerous town squares, markets, and plazas, well over 2,000 apartment buildings, and perhaps most significantly, over 600 pyramids believed to have been used for religious purposes. Though various districts of the city appear to have provided housing for influential individuals from across the Teotihuacano sphere of influence, scholars note the absence of fortifications and military installations, which suggests they had a peaceful co-existence with their neighbors. Believed to have reached its pinnacle by 450 A.D., this massive city, which covered nearly 12 square miles, seems to have represented a culture of unprecedented power whose sphere of influence extended some 10,000 square miles across much of Mesoamerica, as far south as Guatemala.

Widely known as a center of industry and trade, Teotihuacán maintained a large artistic sector that was full of potters, jewelers, and craftsmen recognized for exquisite obsidian goods. But after thriving for perhaps 650 years, the city faced a drastic decline, with invaders from the north conquering and burning down the palaces, temples, and places used by the upper classes. Scholars still debate whether the invaders were the Toltec themselves or whether the Toltec simply rose to prominence by waiting for Teotihuacán to disintegrate.

The ruins of Teotihuacán

While modern scholars debate the extent and degree of Teotihuacano influence - with some believing they maintained militaristic dominance and others believing that adoption of foreign traits was part of their cultural modus operandi - there seems little doubt that the city of Teotihuacán had a major influence on the Late Preclassic and Classic Maya (400 B.C. – 100 A.D. and 250-900 A.D. respectively). This may have been accomplished by the conquest of a number of Maya centers, including Tikal and the region of Peten; hieroglyphic inscriptions made by the Maya describe their encounters with Teotihuacano conquerors. It's also widely believed that the Teotihuacano influenced the Toltec, and thus the Aztec and Yaqui cultures indirectly, regardless of whether the Toltec conquered the Teotihuacano or not.

According to Aztec oral and written history, the Mexica (the Aztec protogroup) originated in Aztlán, a place generally assumed to have been located somewhere north of the Valley of Mexico. However, many historians think the Mexica may have originated as far north as the U.S. Southwest. The Mexica were a Nahuatl-speaking group thought to have included the Chichimeca peoples, who were actually many different groups with varying ethnic and linguistic affiliations that adopted the Aztec designation after the founding of Tenochtitlan and the Aztec empire. Based on Aztec codices and other regional histories, the Mexica arrived at Chapultepec (in modern-day Mexico City) around 1248 A.D., and at that time, Chapultepec was formerly a

Teotihuacano settlement and currently a Toltec one.

At the time of their arrival, the Valley of Mexico had many city-states competing for resources, the most powerful of which was the Culhuacan culture to the south and the Azcapotzalco culture to the west. After the Mexica were expelled from Azcapotzalco, presumably for their barbaric habits, in 1299, the Culhuacan ruler Cocoxtli gave the Mexica permission to settle in the barren reaches of Tizapan, where they are thought to have assimilated Culhuacan culture. According to legend, in 1323 the Mexica were directed by a vision to a small swampy island in Lake Texcoco, where by 1325 they founded Tenochtitlan as the heart of what became the Aztec empire.

At first, Tenochtitlan was officially a satellite of Azcapotzalco, which at the time was a regional power. But during a regional power play, the so-called Triple Alliance was formed by the rulers of Tenochtitlan, Texcoco, and Tlacopan, who proceeded to defeat Azcapotzalco in 1428. For the next century, the Alliance dominated the Valley of Mexico, slowly extending its power base to the Gulf of Mexico and west to the Pacific Ocean. During this time, Tenochtitlan gradually became the dominant power within the alliance, and thus the Aztec became the dominant civilization. Though still officially part of the Triple Alliance, the Aztec systematically imposed their political hegemony far beyond the Valley of Mexico, supplanting local customs with their complex mythological, religious, architectural and artistic traditions and effectively establishing themselves as imperial rulers. During their rise to power, the Aztec would claim descent from the Toltec, and in some cases, they claimed to have defeated the Toltec in early battles. The Aztec claimed to have usurped the Toltec's social and religious institutions (including their gods), incorporated sacred Toltec lands into their own, and promoted what are now widely believed to be exaggerated or even fabricated accounts of Toltec accomplishments to bolster their own cultural standing in the region.

With the Aztec Empire reaching its height of power during the reign of Ahuitzotl (1486–1502), Ahuitzotl's successor, Motehcuzōma Xocoyotzin (better known to history as Montezuma), had ruled the Aztecs for 19 years when Spanish conquistador Hernán Cortés arrived with an army of Spaniards and a large group of Nahuatl-speaking indigenous allies. Cortés proceeded to attack Tenochtitlan and after defeating the Triple Alliance under the leadership of Montezuma, he established Spanish rule over Mexico. Although the population of Tenochtitlan remained largely intact, a smallpox epidemic in 1520 and another in 1576 brought about a decline in the Valley of Mexico's indigenous population by more than 80% over the course of about six decades.

Today, Aztec culture and history (and by association, that of the Toltec) is known primarily through archaeological evidence, such as that uncovered at Templo Mayor, one of the main temples in the capital city of Tenochtitlan. Other evidence has been gleaned from indigenous bark paper codices (accounts written by the Aztec before the arrival of the Spanish), part of which are commonly referred to as the Aztec Chronicles. Then there are also primary sources consisting of firsthand written accounts by Cortés and Bernal Díaz del Castillo, soldiers fighting for Spain, and 16th and 17th century descriptions written by Spanish clergy and literate Aztec. Perhaps the most famous and reliable account is the Florentine Codex, which was compiled by Franciscan monk Bernardino de Sahagún from information provided by Aztec interlocutors.

Chapter 3: The Aztec Chronicles

Prior to scholarly examinations of the so-called Aztec Chronicles, the Aztec oral and pictographic tradition relating the history and culture of the Toltec Empire was widely viewed as myth. For centuries, it was simply presumed the Toltec was an Aztec invention created for the purpose of claiming a distinguished heritage. Although there is no doubt that there is a large mythological component to the Aztec narrative, scholars remain divided as to whether the Chronicles should be considered descriptions of actual events or just fantastical imaginings, and many consider the accounts to be more than mere romanticized legend. These scholars contend that by applying critical comparative methodology, fact can be separated from fable.

Scholarly dialogue regarding the nature of the Toltec culture began in earnest in the late 19th century, after Mesoamerican scholars Francisco Clavigero, Manuel Orozco y Berra, and Charles Etienne Brasseur de Bourbourg studied the Aztec Chronicles and asserted they were actually historic descriptions of a pan-Mesoamerican empire based at Tula. This view quickly came under scrutiny by archaeologist Daniel Garrison Brinton, who argued that the Toltec described in the Aztec narrative were merely one of several Nahuatl-speaking city-states in the Postclassic period and not particularly significant to the Mesoamerican historical picture. He attributed the Aztec perception of the Toltec as a "natural tendency of the human mind to glorify the good-old days" and the "confounding of the place of Tollan with the myth of the struggle between Quetzalcoatl and Tezcatlipoca."[9] But Brinton's dismissive views were subsequently rejected by French archaeologist Claud Joseph Désiré Charnay, who worked at the Toltec site of Tula and the Maya site of Chichén Itzá (in Yucatan) and noted extraordinary similarities in architectural styles between the two sites. This led him to theorize that Chichén Itzá had been violently taken over by a Toltec military force under the leadership of Kukulcan.

As the debates continued, the historicist school of thought continued to gain academic support into the 20th century, and scholars began to associate the Toltec with the Late Classic (700-900), early Postclassic period (900-1000), and the Postclassic Maya civilizations of Chichén Itzá, Mayapán, and the Guatemalan Highlands. Some scholars have even referred to these periods as Toltecized or Mexicanized Maya. By the 1940s, a number of anthropologists and historians came to specialize in Nahuatl thought and literature, including Miguel León Portilla, Nigel Davies, and H. B. Nicholson, all of whom maintained that the Toltec were an actual cultural group associated with the modern-day archaeological site of Tula, believed to have been the Toltec capital city of Tollán in Aztec legend. Noted French archaeologist Laurette Sejourné has even argued that the original Tollán was probably Teotihuacán.

---

[9] *Brinton, Daniel Garrison. Were the Toltecs an Historic Nationality?*

According to the historicist view, between the 10th and 12th century, much of Central Mexico was dominated by the Toltec Empire (though not all agree on the empire designation), and while the peak period of Tollán and Toltec influence was relatively short lived, lasting perhaps from 900-1100, the city of Tollán itself spanned an area of over nine square miles. According to Mesoamerican anthropologist Robert Cobean, Tollán "had a complex socioeconomic structure with a highly developed social, economic, and political institutions, and a population in the tens of thousands."[10]

While 20th century Aztec scholars like Henry B. Nicholson and Nigel Davies sought to glean historic data from the Aztec Chronicles by comparing the various narratives, which were essentially varying accounts of Toltec rulers and their exploits, others considered the Aztec accounts too convoluted to accurately separate fact from fantasy. Meanwhile, Aztec historians Michel Graulich and Susan D. Gillespie offered the perspective that the Chronicles should be viewed as reflective of the Aztec's cyclical perception of time, whereby events repeat themselves at the beginning and end of cycles. Using the two Toltec rulers commonly identified with the god Quetzalcoatl, the first being Ce Acatl Topiltzin (a valiant warrior credited with founding the Toltec dynasty) and the last being Huemac (a feeble and self-doubting old man who saw the end of Toltec glory and was forced into exile in disgrace), Graulich and Gillespie suggest that the Aztec cyclical view was being applied to the historical record, thus making it impossible to distinguish between a historical Ce Acatl Topiltzin and the deity Quetzalcoatl. Graulich subsequently resigned himself to the idea that the only reliable historical data in the Chronicles are the names of some of the rulers, and perhaps some of the conquests ascribed to them.

Conversely, a number of other Mesoamerican scholars discredit the Aztec accounts on the basis that claims of Toltec ancestry and a ruling dynasty founded by Quetzalcoatl have been made not only by the Aztec but the Quiché and Itza' Maya of the Guatemala Highlands. Furthermore, linguists question if Tollán was actually the capital of the Toltec Empire as suggested by the Aztec accounts, arguing it is more likely that the term Toltec simply referred to any inhabitant of Tollán during its peak. These linguists assert that separating the historical Toltec from the Aztec accounts requires further discovery of archaeological clues to the ethnicity, history, and social organization of the inhabitants of Tollán, who were clearly diverse in ethnicity and included non-Nahuatl-speaking peoples.

Chapter 4: The Toltec Historical Picture

According to the archaeological record, civilization began in Mesoamerica at various locations between 2700-1700 B.C., when semi-nomadic indigenous peoples began settling farming communities. By all indications, once the settlement process began, within just a few centuries, a major independent culture arose from the low lands of Veracruz and Tabasco (on the Gulf Coast of Mexico), emerging as the Olmec. The Olmec civilization produced corn/maize, squash, and

---

[10] *Cobean, Robert H.* The Coyotlatelco Culture and the Origins of the Toltec State.

other plant foods in such quantities that they were afforded the manpower to build great monuments and ceremonial centers. Culturally-speaking, their pyramids, open plazas, and human-sacrificial centers are thought to have established the model subsequent societies like the Zapotec, Teotihuacano, Maya, Toltec, and Aztec would emulate. Proving to be one of the most enduring societal models yet known, the cultural structure the Olmec established lasted for about 3,000 years.

The cultural evolution that took place in Mesoamerica prior to the arrival of Europeans is extraordinary by any measure. Evidence of pottery making appears in the fossil record by 2000 B.C., and science and technology became motivational factors for many cultures, initially for spiritual significance. Art, for example, quickly evolved from simple referential imagery to writing, with texts varying in form and complexity according to time, specific culture, and language. No true alphabet was ever developed for these early forms of writing, making decipherment tricky even for modern linguists. Other art forms involved not just the graphic (used to express ideological concepts or features of nature) but the monumental (the advent of flat-topped pyramids thought by many historians to have spawned the so-called moundbuilding traditions found across North America). It's unclear which cultures came up with innovations like metalworking, astronomy, arithmetic, the calendar, and advanced irrigation techniques, because the overlap of the Maya, Teotihuacano, Toltec, and Aztec make it almost impossible to discern who to credit with cultural advances.

For many Mesoamerican scholars, the "Maya factor" - the historic rise and fall of the Maya civilization in Mesoamerica - is critical to understanding the emergence of the Toltec people, as well as their subsequent rise to power and ultimate demise. A number of theories connect the Toltec and Maya cultures, with some arguing the Toltec emerged from the Maya people and others suggesting that the Toltec's regional domination came about by conquering the Maya. What these have in common is the belief that understanding the Toltec's culture cannot be accomplished without a clear understanding of the Maya. Though clearly interdependent, the relationship between these two powerful cultures remains a matter of debate.

By all indications, the Maya civilization of Central Mexico reached its full power by early in the 8th century, just as the Teotihuacano city of Teotihuacán was in final decline. However, within a century and a half, most cities of this area suffered decline, followed by collapse and abandonment. This Terminal Classic Period (800-925) was a time of unprecedented tragedy for the region's inhabitants, but ironically, the Maya managed to exert incomparable influence over the Gulf Coast and Central Highlands of Mexico, with Chichén Itzá and the Puuk region in the Northern Area thriving as never before. It was a time of both upheaval and new stability for the Maya people, as the dominant ruling class in the south fell from grace while a new political order was forming in the north. As a result, southern cities were disintegrating while northern cities were experiencing unprecedented prosperity, and the area of Central Mexico where the Teotihuacano had recently held sway saw the migration of untold numbers of Maya. This ensured that the two cultures ultimately became intertwined, and it was apparently from this cultural landscape that the Toltec emerged as an independent culture and rose to power.

After nearly two centuries piecing together the Toltec historical picture, based primarily on Spanish accounts written nearly four centuries after the fact and the Aztec Chronicles, most scholars now believe the Toltec became a force to be reckoned with by 900. Having formerly lived as a semi-nomadic and possibly warlike people in western and northern Mexico, the first Toltec arrived in Mesoamerica under the leadership of Mixcoatl (Cloud Serpent), sacking and instigating the ultimate collapse of the Teotihuacano city of Teotihuacán. Archaeological and other historical evidence suggests that Teotihuacán had reached its peak of power by 500 but had begun to deteriorate by 70, making it incapable of resisting outside forces. As renowned American archaeologist and Teotihuacán authority Rene Million explains, "The military is most prominently represented at Teotihuacan between AD 650 and 750 . . . . This may be both a symptom of difficulty and a cause of [its demise]."[11]

While his role is not completely understood, Ce Acatl Topiltzin (who may have been Mixcoatl's son) is credited with building Tollán upon the ruins of Teotihuacán and thus founding the Toltec Empire. Better known as Quetzalcoatl, or "Feathered Serpent", Ce Acatl Topiltzin is by far the most famous hero-god in Mesoamerican history. By the time the Toltec seized control of Teotihuacán around 800 (this date is highly speculative), the capital city had been deteriorating for at least a century, but a substantial portion of the population, possibly tens of thousands, continued to reside there. Although the Teotihuacano culture had long since collapsed, its four principal economic assets remained in place. It had rich obsidian deposits, particularly the highly-coveted green obsidian from Pachuca. The city also sat midstream and was a natural trade route connecting the Basin of Mexico to points south and east (the Gulf Coast). Furthermore, the Teotihuacan Valley offered enormous potential for intensified agriculture via irrigation, and though the original significance had been lost to time, Teotihuacán held great religious standing among the indigenous groups of the region. It's even possible that it was a religious center that drew pilgrims to it as well. Thus, it appears that through coercion and a minimal show of military power, the Toltec were able to essentially move in and assume control of Teotihuacano state business.

---

[11] *Sabloff, Jeremy A.* The Cities of Ancient Mexico: Reconstructing a Lost World. *Page 68.*

Aztec depiction of Quetzalcoatl as a feathered serpent

According to Aztec accounts, around 987, a struggle ensued between Toltec Emperor Ce Actl Topiltzin and his loyal followers against the Toltec warrior sector, comprised of the Eagle, Jaguar, and Coyote orders that represented Tezcatlipoca, the god of war. Ultimately defeated by Tezcatlipoca's dark magick, Ce Acatl Topiltzin was forced to leave Tollán in disgrace, and he and his followers were said to have made their way to the Gulf Coast, where they set out on rafts to reestablish Quetzalcoatl's domain. According to corresponding Maya accounts, a man from the west calling himself K'uk'ulkan (Feathered Serpent) arrived that same year, "wrested Yucatan from its rightful owners and established his capital at Chichén Itzá."[12] But as Maya scholar Ralph Roys cautions, the accounts of this supposed event are seriously confused with the history of a later people called the Itza, who moved into the Yucatan in the 13th century and subsequently added their name to the former Chich'en.

Graphically rendered on the Temple of the Warriors at Chichén Itzá, the Maya account describes the Toltec under K'uk'ulkan as arriving by sea along the Campeche shore, prompting

---

[12] *Coe, Michael D.* The Maya. *Page 167.*

Maya warriors to row out on rafts to confront them. Losing the sea battle, the fighting then resumed on land, with the Maya army defeated once again. After the Toltec seized a major Maya settlement, Maya leaders decided to surrender, and their hearts were literally sacrificed to the Feathered Serpent, who by their description "hovered above to receive the bloody offering."

Many historians discount the Maya account of an invasion by the peace-loving Quetzalcoatl or question the interpretation of the wall rendering, but others point out that several Toltec architectural techniques were subsequently incorporated by the Maya during the Puuc phase, which ended around 1000. For example, Tollánic-style columns were commonly used in place of room dividers, a Toltec method of utilizing space, and Tollánic colonnades were incorporated into a number of Maya structures, including low masonry banquettes that depicted processions of Toltec warriors and feathered serpent motifs. Additionally, a syncretism of Maya and Toltec ideology is apparent in subsequent Maya motifs, where members of the Toltec Jaguar and Eagle orders are depicted along with men dressed in traditional Maya garb, and Toltec deities sit with Maya gods.

A feathered serpent sculpture found at Chichén Itzá

Although the debate continues as to whether the Toltec ever staged an invasion of Chichén Itzá or other Maya cities, a melding of ideas clearly took place at some point, after which the traditional Maya order was replaced with a Toltec-Maya hybrid. This is perhaps no better illustrated than at the aptly-named Castillo, the great four-sided temple-pyramid at Chichén Itzá dedicated to the K'uk'ulkan (Feathered Serpent) cult.

El Castillo at Chichén Itzá has a "serpent effect", during which the sun's rays create the appearance of a serpent at certain times.

Some have argued that if the Toltec descended from the Maya, they would have a shared system of iconography, but the Temple of Warriors at Chichén Itzá, located across from the Castillo, is an aggrandized replica of the pyramid at Tollán. Its size is said to symbolize Toltec ascendancy over Yucatan, and the chacmool figure commonly found across Mesoamerica and Maya sites is thought to have been Toltec in origin.

The Temple of Warriors with the chacmool figure

Conclusions regarding the apparent Toltec-Maya relationship have historically been presented by individual Maya or Toltec scholars working from limited information that is by no means accepted as reliable by all scholars. Therefore, conclusions drawn from such works are generally accepted as possible but not necessarily probable. Even as more definitive data regarding these groups become available, scholars frequently disagree as to the nature of the relationship between the Toltec, Aztec and Maya.

The first significant breakthrough regarding the well-known but wholly enigmatic Toltec occurred in the 1940s, when Mexican archaeologists Wigberto Jimenez Moreno and Jorge R. Acosta identified Tula as the Toltec capital city of Tollán after years of painstaking research. Stylistic motifs that ultimately enabled Moreno and Acosta to distinguish Toltec from Teotihuacano iconography were largely military in nature, including representations of the Jaguar and Eagle military orders holding prominent positions, death and blood featured all over the place, and eagles devouring hearts depicted prominently.

Image depicting a Toltec ruler found at Tollán

From 1961-1964, American archaeologist and noted Mesoamerican scholar Richard A. Diehl worked in the Teotihuacan Valley and the Aztec's capital city of Teotihuacán under renowned archaeologist William T. Sanders. Subsequently, Diehl argued for the existence of a Toltec archaeological horizon, a sphere of influence characterized by certain stylistic traits and motifs associated with Tollán that extended to other cultures and cities of Mesoamerica. These included the presence of Mixteca-Puebla style iconography (an artistic style and iconography commonly found on pottery that became associated with the Toltec but also found in the Maya walled city of Tulum), Tohil plumbate ceramic ware (thought to have been first produced near southwest Guatemala), and Silho Orange Ware ceramics, which were uncovered in Aguacatal. Of course, there are also several stylistic traits associated with Tollán found at Chichén Itzá as well.

Toltec orange colored pottery

In 1983, archaeologist Robert H. Cobean began a project called "Tula y Su Area Directa de Interaccionnes" ("Tula and its Direct Area of Interactions"), aimed at investigating the origins, development, and expansion of the Toltec state. Using the region's Coyotlatelco population for comparison (a culture contemporary with the Toltec and identifiable by their distinctive figurine style), Cobean and his team conducted large-scale excavations of residential structures, with particular concentration on workshops and high activity areas. Since Coyotlatelco stone tools were routinely produced from rhyolite and basalt materials, while the Toltec utilized the more exotic obsidian, Cobean was able to create a more definitive timeline, determining the periods of maximum urban expansion and population growth, as well as a measure of social and economic complexity.

Cobean's findings supported many commonly-held assumptions about the rise and fall of the Toltec culture, but they also refuted others. For scholars who had envisioned the Toltec as a warring people who had taken the Teotihuacano city of Teotihuacán by force, Cobean's findings were disappointing. Physical evidence indicates that nearly all Teotihuacán-associated sites had been abandoned by 750, a reality directly related to Teotihuacán's decline as a political and economic center. Moreover, this decline brought about radical changes throughout Central Mexico that further affected population distribution, subsequent settlement patterns, political and economic relationships, and prompted the development of numerous regional centers. These centers were often established on hilltops or positions easily defended, indicative of the instability of the region and the nature of conflict among different groups. Moreover, the appearance of new ceramics styles in the fossil record, coupled with new styles in architecture and artistic motifs, seem to indicate an influx of new ethnic groups to the region or, at a minimum, radical changes within the groups already established.

By the time Cobean began surveying Tula and the ruins of Tollán located there, it had become generally accepted that the Coyotlatelco had played a pivotal role in the decline of the Teotihuacán state and the subsequent rise of the Toltec (at Tollán). Although their participation was far from understood, their presence across several centuries seemed to support the contention that were they not somehow complicit or influential, they could not have survived the turmoil of this period. Cobean's findings, however, shed new light on this culture, as well as the development of the Toltec state. Upon examination of three key Coyotlatelco habitation sites, it became apparent that by the final phase of Teotihuacán's decline, aside from than the highly-complex urban site of Tula Chico (located near Cerro Magoni on the Tula River), the majority of Coyotlatelco most likely occupied large hilltop settlements, constituting political and economic units independent of Teotihuacano control. Cobean hypothesized that Tula Chico was actually settled by people (perhaps Coyotlatelco and/or remnants of the Teotihuacán-related population) who moved down from the hilltop communities and subsequently experienced a social, economic, and political boon that drew many of the region's scattered inhabitants. According to Cobean, Tula Chico clearly constitutes the first stage of the subsequent Tollán metropolis phase, further suggesting that the legendary struggle between Toltec leader Ce Acatl Topiltzin and Teotihuacano leader Tezcatlipoca may have taken place in Tula Chico's main plaza. This would also explain why it was subsequently abandoned despite its prime location within the thriving city.

Lastly, Cobean's work addressed the question of whether Tollán should be considered a state at all. According to sociological criteria, to constitute a state, a society must be divided according to classes and governed by a central ruling group who controls production, distribution, and consumption of resources. Other accepted state attributes include territoriality, a highly-developed religious system that promotes the ideology and worldview legitimizing political and economic control, and institution of a coercive mechanism (like police or military) accepted as a reasonable means by which to maintain societal cohesion and compliance. On each of these measures, Cobean asserts that the Tollánic sphere of influence did not meet these criteria, writing, "We believe that [Tula's political and economic influence] did not extend very far beyond Tula's immediate hinterland . . . . The center of the state was located outside the Tula area and an enormous metropolis in the Basin of Mexico. During the decline of Teotihuacan the

Coyotlatelco culture emerged in the Tula region. The initial Coyotlatelco settlements, however, did not constitute and were not part of a state. Among these settlements there is no one large center that clearly dominated and controlled the entire area. In terms of social and economic complexity . . . these settlements possess some degree of socioeconomic stratification but lack developed classes and . . . other political institutions."13

In the wake of Richard Diehl's early 1960s argument for the existence of a Toltec archaeological horizon connecting the Toltec and other Mesoamerican cultures, the nature of the interaction between Tollán and Chichén Itzá became a highly contentious issue, with scholars arguing for either military conquest of Chichén Itzá by the Toltec, Chichén Itzá establishing Tollán as a colony, or for a much more casual but cooperative connection between the two. In 2003, following studies conducted by Arizona State University archaeologists Michael E. Smith and Lisa Montiel comparing the archaeological record of Tollán to those of Teotihuacán and the Aztec city-state of Tenochtitlan, the two concluded that relative to the influence exerted in Mesoamerica by the other key centers, Tollán's influence on other cultures was negligible and probably not deserving of being defined as an empire but more like a kingdom. While Tollán did have the urban complexity of an imperial capital, with the remains of a large obsidian workshop thought to reflect extensive trade networks, its influence and dominance was not very far reaching. In their formal paper, they wrote, "The hegemonic-type empires of ancient Mesoamerica are difficult to study archaeologically because they left fewer material traces than more territorially organized empires such as the Inka or similar cases. Empires can be identified from three types of evidence: characteristics of the capital city, evidence for varying types of political domination of provincial areas, and examples of the projection of influence in a larger, international context. We apply this model to archaeological data on three central Mexican cases—Tenochtitlan, Teotihuacan, and Tula. The results suggest that both Tenochtitlan and Teotihuacan ruled empires, whereas Tula did not."14

Chapter 5: The Toltec Religion

While little can be stated with absolute certainty regarding Toltec spiritual beliefs, it is generally accepted that Toltec iconography reflects both political and spiritual concepts, and while ethnographic accounts collected by early Spanish clergy via Aztec interlocutors enliven the iconography found throughout Toltec ruins, most scholars agree that the Aztec viewed history as malleable and something to be manipulated. This casts at least some doubt on any understanding of the Toltec religion.

With that said, the Spanish journal entries of the 16th century indicate that two deities held prominent places in the Toltec pantheon of gods: Quetzalcoatl (the Feathered Serpent and

---

[13] *Cobean, Robert H.* The Coyotlatelco Culture and the Origins of the Toltec State.

[14] *Smith Michael E., and Lisa Montiel.* The Archaeological Study of Empires and Imperialism in Pre-Hispanic Central Mexico.

Morning Star) and Tezcatlipoca (the god of war). The worship of a feathered serpent deity has been traced to Teotihuacán as far back as the 1st century A.D., and veneration of that figure is thought to have spread throughout Mesoamerica by the Late Classic period, 600-900 A.D.

Tezcatlipoca depicted as a jaguar in a 16th century codex

In the era following the Spanish conquest, a number of sources conflate Quetzalcoatl with Ce Acatl Topiltzin, the legendary founder of Tollán and the Toltec people. Subsequently becoming one of several important deities in the Aztec pantheon, Quetzalcoatl was associated with gods of the wind, the planet Venus, dawn, merchants, arts & crafts, and acquisition of knowledge. He was also the patron god of the Aztec priesthood, representing learning and sacred knowledge. Meanwhile, the well-known Tezcatlipoca figure, usually depicted with a black and yellow stripe painted across his face, dates to the Olmec occupational period (1700-400 B.C.) and appears to have remained a primary deity for the Maya and Aztec, becoming associated with the earth, the night sky, night winds, hurricanes, the direction north, obsidian, divination, jaguars, sorcery, beauty, and war.

Another figure prominently displayed throughout Tollán and other sites of Toltec influence (including the Maya site of Chichén Itzá) is known as a chacmool, a reclining sculptured figure with an offering plate on its stomach long speculated to have been designed to hold hearts removed from sacrificial victims. That said, it appears the Toltec maintained an obsession with what has been regarded as the Toltec warrior, a figure with a pillbox-like headdress with a downward-flying bird in front, a highly stylized bird or butterfly on his chest, and armed with a feather-decorated atlatl in one hand (a spear-thrower device consisting of a shaft with a cup at the end that supports and propels the dart) and a cache of darts in the other. Historians are divided as to whether this figure represents a typical Toltec warrior or the mythical warrior ideal.

Relief sculptures at Tollán depicting jaguars, coyotes and eagles eating hearts

From many historical perspectives, it is Toltec religious rites that most objectively set them apart from earlier Mesoamerican civilizations. Frequently characterized as ruthless and bloodthirsty, based on the presumed military domination used to seize control of the Valley of Mexico and the violent art and monumental works thought to reflect their spiritual worldview, historians often credit the Toltec with normalizing the element of human sacrifice practiced by both the Maya and Aztec. Controversy surrounds which cultural group affected which, but physical evidence indicates that the Toltec were indeed obsessed with death. How that obsession manifested itself in Toltec society beyond symbolism and art remains a matter of debate, but many scholars insist they practiced ritual blood-letting, heart-removal, and perhaps decapitation. According to testimony gathered by the Spanish and Jesuit historians after seizing control of the Aztec capital of Tenochtitlan, religion among the Mesoamericans was based on the belief that the gods had sacrificed their blood for the creation of mankind, so man was obliged to sacrifice human blood in kind. Accordingly, large-scale public sacrifices took place, often on the steps of temple pyramids, as demonstrations of religious devotion.

The rites of sacrifice common in the region had a priest or ruler dressed as a god or goddess — thus temporarily becoming that deity - accompanied by a band of musicians, officiate over ceremonies that celebrated the power of the gods. The rites reenacted the primal scenes of divine sacrifice through which humans and the Sun first came into existence. Oral history of the region asserts that ritual slaughter had reached a new peak near the end of the collapse of Tollán, but it is widely believed that the Temple of the Feathered Serpent at Chichén Itzá was dedicated and perhaps built to accommodate ritual sacrifice. Oral tradition speaks of a time when huge crowds, including cadres of visiting dignitaries, gathered en masse to form awe-inspiring assemblages of religious aspirants whose cheers rose high into the heavens as human blood (and by some accounts, human heads) flowed down the temple steps. Alligators, jaguar, and other animals were also sacrificed according to some accounts.

If Aztec accounts are to be taken as history, incense, music, and dancing were integral elements of all Toltec rituals. Incense (usually copal resin, but also rubber and chicle tree resin) was thought to become food for the gods as it rose into the air, with resin sometimes shaped to replicate animal hearts when the actual organs were not available for sacrifice. Reportedly, large groups of musicians took part in all sacred events, including processions and ceremonies, by playing instruments crafted of clay, shell, and gourds. Their drums, horns, rattles, and instruments imitated animal calls. Holding special rank among the people of Tollán, dance troupes took part in all public ceremonies and ritual sacrifice as well, conducting sacred dances for special occasions (like preparing for war) and sometimes performing priest-like functions.

Chapter 6: Tollán

The available evidence suggests Tollán did not rise to prominence until about 800, decades after the fall of Teotihuacán, and it reached its peak of influence by 900 before losing its hold by 1100. Ceramic and other artifact analysis indicates a rapid population increase proportional to the decline of Teotihuacán, coupled with the introduction of thousands of immigrants from north and west Mexico. Physical evidence further indicates that Tollán never reached the size of Teotihuacán and never exceeded 9 square miles in size, suggesting its maximum population was between 35,000-60,000. As a result, many believe the city exerted little control beyond the city proper and ultimately never reached the level of influence that Teotihuacán had.

Piecing together the archaeological evidence, along with Spanish references and cross-cultural oral accounts, Toltec life at Tollán was much less organized than that of subsequent or even previous Mesoamerican cultures. Tollán was laid out in what can best be characterized as a haphazard, seemingly lackadaisical manner, with residential areas clustered together in a way that suggested there was little apparent planning. These areas were surrounded by a variety of courtyards, alleys, houses, and storage structures built side-by-side. The well-known Acropolis Zone, the location of the Temple of Quetzalcoatl, is perhaps the one exception to the seeming lack of planning. Nonetheless, the Toltec are credited with inventing several architectural innovations, including monumental porticoes, distinctive serpent columns, gigantic Atlantean statues (carved-stone support pillars in the shape of fierce men), human and animal standard bearers, and what are perhaps their most identifiable feature, the reclining Chac-Mool (also chacmool) figures.

Photo of columns and a ball court in the distance at Tollán, by Susana Torres Sánchez

Atlantean statues representing Toltec warriors found at Tollán

A chacmool found at Chichén Itzá

Throughout the city of Tollán were a number of centers where craftsmen manufactured various goods, including ceramics, obsidian tools, cotton textiles, and stone bowls, all of which were reflective of an economy at least partially based on trade. There is little question that Tollán also represented a large agricultural center. The presence of a variety of pottery types native to distant Central America destinations suggest trade across the region and/or frequent visitors to the city, and most Mesoamerican scholars believe Tollán had widespread contacts throughout Mexico, deep into the frontier areas to the north and south. Unquestionably, much of Tollán's trade clout hinged on their access to obsidian, used in pottery, the manufacture of blades, and even the crafting of mirrors, handicrafts, and various ritual items. Additionally, they are thought to have held a monopoly on a rare green obsidian found in the Pachuca region.

Militarily speaking, it had long been assumed that the Toltec had conquered the city of Teotihuacán and therefore represented a formidable military force. This perspective was for centuries perpetuated by the Spanish, who benefited from portraying the Aztec as a powerful, warrior race who themselves had claimed descent from great Toltec warriors. While it can be assumed that the countless depictions of death and military symbolism found throughout Tollán and other Toltec centers is indicative of military prowess (they unquestionably had a considerable army at the ready), the role the military played in Toltec society is far from understood. Additionally, with modern scholarship largely playing down the notion that there was a big Toltec military expansion, there is little to suggest that military might was directly relevant to establishing or maintaining control of Tollán or other areas of the region where they may have wielded influence.

That said, some evidence suggests that by 900, the Toltec used Tollán as a base of operation to conduct regular raids on neighboring indigenous groups. Intermarriage with neighboring cultures like the Zapotec and Miztec was changing the ethnic makeup of the surrounding population as well, which almost certainly affected the Toltec. Some scholars believe the Teotihuacano themselves were an amalgamation of Zapotec and Miztec peoples, or were at least greatly influenced by their unique farming and irrigation techniques.

During the late-11th century, Tollán, now under the reign of Emperor Huemac, began sustaining waves of attacks from the barbarous Chicimec people, of which the Aztec are thought to have been a subgroup. According to popular lore, Huemac was a corrupt ruler whose self-centered nature had sentenced the Toltec people to six years of plagues by the tlaloques, the rain god's representatives on Earth. After Tollán had suffered untold crop-destroying frosts, droughts, floods, and storms, Huemac abdicated his throne, seating his illegitimate son Acxitl in his place. Acxitl, however, proved even more corrupt than his father, prompting two outlying provinces to send armies led by a nobleman named Huehuetzin to seize control of the capital city. The armies were ultimately bought off with Tollán's riches, but word spread that the Toltec people had no worthy defender. A short time later, the opportunistic Chicimec flooded into Toltec territory, defeating the Toltec army and then occupying Tollán and other Toltec cities. The relationship between the Chicimec and Aztec is not entirely clear, but many scholars believe it was the Aztec - at that point a relatively small, barbaric and semi-nomadic group - that ultimately seized control of Tollán.)

In the aftermath of the fall of Tollán, a political free-for-all ensued throughout Central Mexico, with emigrating Toltec moving south from the capital city into the Mexican Basin, along with other groups of the north and west seeking stability. Settling into small intertribal city-states scattered throughout the Basin, a competition for power and resources ensued, with many groups coalescing for power. Finally, towards the end of the 13th century, the main body of Mexica/Aztec arrived, at first serving as mercenaries for the large city-state of Colhuacan. According to the Aztec codices, the Mexica arrived at Chapultepec around 1248, a time in which Chapultepec had already been a Teotihuacano settlement and was now a Toltec settlement. Ultimately seizing control of the region from their stronghold at Tenochtitlan (founded around 1325), the Aztec absorbed Tollán and other Toltec cities into their empire.

Chapter 7: The Toltec and Sorcery

In 1968, Peruvian-born American anthropologist and self-proclaimed shaman Carlos Castaneda published *The Teachings of Don Juan: A Yaqui way of Knowledge*, introducing the world to the philosophy and practices of the Toltec sorcerer don Juan, one of the last members of an elusive band of nagual. The nagual were supposedly humans who (according to Mesoamerican folklore) have the power to magically transform themselves into animal form, especially jaguars and pumas. In *The Teachings*, the first in his now-famous trilogy that included *A Separate Reality* and *Journey to Ixtlan*, Castaneda uses the term Toltec to denote a person who was recruited into this secret society of sorcerers, joining a tradition that had its origin in the Mesoamerican culture of that same name.

In *The Teachings of Don Juan*, Castaneda recounts in narrative style his own indoctrination into the nagual tradition in 1960, relating conversations with his teacher who he refers to as don Juan and sharing the perceptions he experienced during his apprenticeship, which required him to take the hallucinogenic drugs mescalito (peyote), yerba del diablo (datura), and humito (magic mushrooms). But as stated by UCLA professor of anthropology Walter Goldschmidt in the forward of *The Teachings*, "This is no mere recounting of hallucinatory experiences, for don Juan's subtle manipulations have guided the traveler while his interpretations give meaning to the events that we, through the sorcerer's apprentice, have the opportunity to experience."[15] Said to have been born in the Southwest in 1891, don Juan lived in Mexico until 1940 before immigrating to Arizona, where he met Castaneda and accepted him as an apprentice in Yaqui sorcery; an apprenticeship that allegedly lasted until 1965.

Among the perceptions Castaneda claims to have recognized is that knowledge is an illusion of reality (what Hindus term "Maya"), an illusion within which most humans become trapped. Accordingly, among the techniques the Toltec nagual developed were methods by which to escape the erosive effects of this illusion, thus permitting them to transcend the limitations of the normal mind (a concept found in a number of Eastern religions today). By perceiving life as limitless, and with no separation between spirit and corporal form, the nagual are allegedly able to achieve what ordinary people (trapped within the illusion of the mind) perceive as impossible or magical. Thus, in ancient times, the nagual garnered reputations as powerful wizards and sorcerers.

In Castaneda's narrative, nagual don Juan describes the Toltec as a guild of sorcerers that formed in Southern Mexico 10,000 years ago to harness the changes of perception brought about by using a number of psychoactive plants. The primary objective, however, of Toltec sorcerers is to seek a way to prevent the disintegration of the self that normally occurs at the time of death.

---

[15] *Castaneda, Carlos.* The Teachings of Don Juan: A Yaqui Way of Knowledge. *Page 9.*

To achieve this goal, the ancient nagual developed a body of knowledge and techniques by which the sorcerer can transform himself into a high-speed inorganic being with an eternal lifespan. Castaneda makes it clear that his use of the term Toltec in this context is specialized, and not directly equatable with the Toltec people or Toltec culture referred to in oral and written tradition of Mesoamerica. While the nagual tradition is said to have had its beginning in the living Toltec culture, those who are now recruited are chosen for their suitability rather than their ethnic or cultural ties.

According to don Juan, the Toltec people were not a tribe in the traditional sense as presented by Maya and Aztec writings but actually a secret society formed around 750 A.D. by the indigenous Mesoamerican population after the conquest of Teotihuacán. Don Juan claimed the Toltec were dedicated to the practice and preservation of ancient knowledge originating on islands of the Pacific Ocean around the time of the island cultures associated with the Lost Continent of Atlantis. According to some sources, the Maya actually claimed decent from the people of Atlantis, while others associate them with the mythological Pacific culture of Mu. This ancient knowledge was reflected in Toltec art, spiritual science (magick), mathematics, and culture, with Teotihuacán becoming known as the place where men became gods.

When Spanish conquistadors brought Catholicism to Mesoamerica, the Toltec nagual allegedly took their society and secret knowledge underground, eventually carrying it north during several waves of migrations. During these migrations, the knowledge was supposedly dispersed among various Native American groups by roaming shamans and teachers such as the Zero Chiefs (elite holymen known as holders of ancient knowledge) and the Twisted Hairs (an ancient indigenous cult who acquired knowledge from multiple sources and were said to have woven it into a body of valid truth that leads to effective change in life) Said to have foreseen the coming of the Europeans and destructive nature of Christianity, the enlightened nagual disappeared, keeping their knowledge secret but passing it down through the generations until a time when it may serve as a solution to modern human problems.

After Carlos Castaneda's don Juan accounts spawned a number of esoteric spiritual groups, other firsthand accounts of Toltec training and culture were subsequently published. Of particular note are those of Taisha Abelar and Florinda Donner. These accounts complement the insight provided by Castaneda and contain additional information specific to the two women's perspectives and training, and they represent branches of esoteric study prompted specifically by Castaneda's introduction of Yaqui/Toltec shamanism. Abelar was a close associate of Castaneda who mysteriously disappeared shortly after Castaneda's death in 1998, and Donner was an anthropologist who specialized in Native American culture but is best known for her ethnographic work in Venezuela and Brazil, studying the curing or witchcraft practices of native cultures. Both women were members of Castaneda's so-called Sorcerers' Clan. Donner was reported missing 15 years ago.

Chapter 8: The Toltec's Legacy

In the psyche of every modern Mexican lies the legend of the Toltec as ancient heroes who brought civilization to Mexico. Larger than life or mere myth, the Toltec represent the spirit of the Mexican people and are widely considered unequaled masters of all the material, technical, and intellectual refinement that determine civilization. In Mexican and Central American culture, the Toltec are known as the inventors of painting, sculpture, and pictographic writing (glyphs), the builders of magnificent palaces and pyramids, and creators of the stylized mosaics of multicolored feathers that decorated military shields and other public emblems. Their farmers, technicians, and ritual specialists knew the secrets of the Earth and cosmos as no people had before. Yet, by the mid-12th century, Tollán, the epicenter of the Toltec civilization, had crumbled and collapsed, leaving migration as the only solution to salvaging the Toltec culture.

According to tradition, around 1168 A.D., the priest-king (sometimes identified as Huemac and sometimes simply Quetzalcoatl, the Plumed Serpent) fled, with some of his followers flooding into the Valley of Mexico and founding new cities later absorbed by the Aztec Empire. Others may have migrated south to Cholula, which some anthropologists contend was another Toltec city, and others went east and joined the Maya. Following the arrival of the Aztec and then the Spanish conquistadors, the Toltec (in their many guises and subgroups) went into hiding. Some may have ventured north and migrated into the Southwest, as the Yaqui claim.

By absorbing the Toltec culture and all its elements, the Aztec attempted to legitimize their regional standing, their use of militarism and their ritual practices, which were extreme even by Mesoamerican standards. But in honoring the achievements of the Toltec, as represented by Tollán and other Toltec cities, the Aztec not only secured their place in history but unwittingly implanted powerful cultural concepts and constructs that endure to this day. In declaring the Teotihuacano city of Teotihuacan (later Tollán) the actual place the gods had gathered to create the sun and mankind, the Aztec effectively designated Tollán as the most sacred spot on the planet. While it's unclear how sacred the Toltec considered Tollán themselves, their apparent reverence for this location promoted such a powerful religious precept that it was incorporated into the Aztec empire itself. Additionally, Toltec leader Ce Acatl Topiltzin (better known as Quetzalcoatl or Feathered Serpent), who is credited with building Tollán and founding the Toltec Empire, is by far the most famous hero-god in Mesoamerican history. Holding a supreme place in Mesoamerican mythology and spirituality even today, students across the world learn about Quetzalcoatl even today, and the importance his legend had on the events that led to the Spanish conquest of the Aztec.

The Pascua Yaqui continue to claim descent from the ancient Toltec, and while that connection remains debatable, the Yaqui culture itself can be traced back to about 550 A.D., when they first formed family units that gathered wild desert foods, hunted game, and cultivated corn, beans, and squash. Few scholars dispute their descent from the ancient Uto-Azteca people of Mexico, and the Pascua Yaqui might very well represent the most direct cultural link between the people of ancient Tollán and a Native American group.

Although documentation of Yaqui history began as early as 1533 (under Spanish occupation), their precise cultural link with the Toltec remains largely speculative and based primarily on oral tradition. According to the Pascua Yaqui website, "The Pascua Yaqui Indians of Arizona are descendants of the ancient Toltec who occupied a large area of the Southwest and Mexico and today have eight communities in Southern Arizona." But it is their journey from Central Mexico north to the U.S. Southwest that scholars find most intriguing.

According to Spanish accounts gleaned largely from Yaqui and Aztec accounts, by 1414 the Yaqui had emerged in the Valley of Mexico as an autonomous cultural group with its own military. Historians speculate that establishment of a functioning military may have been the minimal criteria for cultural autonomy at this point in time, but soon after the arrival of the Spanish in Aztec country in 1519, general warfare broke out as the Spanish sought to enslave the Yaqui population and force them to join the Spanish army. Following decades of sporadic raids on Yaqui villages, from 1608-1610, the Spanish attacked Yaqui settlements and killed thousands of Yaqui. Seeking a peaceful solution, the Yaqui invited Spanish Jesuit missionaries to live among them, which subsequently resulted in a peace treaty with the Spanish. However, when silver was discovered in the Yaqui River Valley around 1684, the Spanish moved their armies onto sacred Yaqui land to ensure control over the resources. In 1740, the Yaqui staged a revolt, allying with the neighboring Mayo tribe to force the Spanish out of the Valley of Mexico, a struggle that would ultimately continue for the next 190 years.

On September 16, 1810, Catholic priest Miguel Hidalgo y Costilla declared Mexico's independence from Spain, which became official on August 24, 1821 with the signing of the Treaty of Córdoba and the Declaration of Independence of the Mexican Empire. Following decades of revolts staged by various indigenous groups, in 1880 the Mexican Army began the forced removal of the Yaqui, enslaving them and sending many to work on plantations in Yucatan, thereby igniting the first major exodus north. Applying various methods to capture, kill, or force the Yaqui from their settlements, the Mexican government stationed soldiers in Yaqui villages, captured and sold thousand of Yaqui to neighboring tribes, and physically drove thousands more into Mexico's wilderness. Though many Yaqui continued to defend their homelands against the Mexicans, by 1887 the Mayo tribe broke from the alliance, and another smallpox epidemic killed countless more Yaqui. Now reduced from 20,000 to a mere 3,000-4,000 by the early 20th century, in 1910 many of the remaining Yaqui opted to join famed Mexican revolutionist Pancho Villa in Arizona during the Mexican Revolution.

As the Yaqui made their way into lands controlled by the U.S., they quickly became known among neighboring Native American groups for their Deer Dances and their art, including statuary art and unique cultural paintings. The Yaqui tribe began to expand, forming settlements north of Tucson in an area they named Pascua Village, as well as settlements in Guadalupe near Tempe. In 1964, the Pascua Yaqui received 202 acres of desert land where their Native North American identity could be asserted, and on September 18, 1978, they became federally-recognized as the Pascua Yaqui Tribe of Arizona with the official establishment of the Pascua Yaqui Indian Reservation. With this recognition, the Mesoamerican Pascua Yaqui were granted status similar to other Native American groups of the United States, making them eligible for a variety of services under U.S. Federal law due to trust responsibility the United States offers all Native American groups who have suffered land loss.

The Pascua Yaqui Indian Reservation, located in Pima County in the southwestern part of the Tucson metropolitan area of Arizona, sits amidst the suburban communities of Drexel Heights and Valencia West and is adjacent to the eastern section of the Tohono O'odham Indian Reservation (known as the San Xavier Indian Reservation). The reservation spans a land area of almost 2 square miles (about 1200 acres) and is surrounded by richly vegetated, scenic desert that offers recreational and sightseeing opportunities to visitors, including Mt. Lemmon ski area (an hour east of Tucson) and Saguaro National Monument (a few miles north). Other sites include the San Xavier del Bac Mission, Sonoran Desert Museum, and Kitt Peak Observatory.

As of the 2000 census, the resident population of the Pascua Yaqui Indian Reservation is 3,315 individuals, over 90% of whom are registered Native Americans. The Pascua Yaqui reservation community is governed by a chairman, a vice chairman, and a nine-member tribal council, with crime prevention provided by the Pascua Yaqui Tribal Police Department, and fire protection supplied by six full-time firefighters and four reserve volunteers.

Online Resources

Other books about Mesoamerican history by Charles River Editors

Bibliography

Ayala, Elaine. The Maya and Olmec, Living in Tandem. In Latino Life, 04.30.13. Accessed via: http://blog.mysanantonio.com/latinlife/2013/04/the-maya-and-olmec-living-in-tandem/ 09.03.2013.

Baldwin, Neil. Legends of the Plumed Serpent: A Biography of a Mexican God. New York: Public Affairs, 1998.

Brinton, Daniel Garrison. Were the Toltecs an Historic Nationality? Proceedings of the American Philosophical Society 24 (126): 229–241,1887. Accessed via: www.latinamericanstudies.org/toltecs/Toltecs.pdf   08.27.2013.

Carrasco, David. Quetzalcoatl and the Irony of Empire: Myths and Prophecies in the Aztec Tradition. Chicago: University of Chicago Press, 1982.

Castaneda, Carlos. The Teachings of Don Juan: A Yaqui Way of Knowledge. CA: University of California Press, 1968.

Cobean, Robert H. The Coyotlatelco Culture and the Origins of the Toltec State. Accessed via: http://books.google.com/books?hl=en&lr=&id=FLJxLlGkpiUC&oi=fnd&pg=PA49&dq=The+Toltec&ots=XVgAJNAiaO&sig=0HYFi2qyXo5X7Tz5bidozhHRG_U#v=onepage&q=The%20Toltec&f=false 08.27.2013.

Coe, Michael D. The Maya. New York: Thames and Hudson, Inc., 1966.

Campbell, Lyle, and Terrence Kaufman. A Linguistic Look at the Olmec. In American Antiquity 41(1):80--89, 1976. Accessed via: http://saa.org/AbouttheSociety/Publications/AmericanAntiquity/tabid/124/Default.aspx 09.04.2013.

Coe, Michael D. The Maya. New York: Thames and Hudson, Inc., 1966.

America's First Civilization: Discovering the Olmec. New York: The Smithsonian Library, 1968.

Cyphers, Ann. From Stone to Symbols: Olmec Art in Social Context at San Lorenzo Tenochtitlán. In Social Patterns in Pre-Classic Mesoamerica. Dumbarton Oaks, Washington, D.C., pp. 155—181, 1999.

Diehl, Richard A. The Olmecs: America's First Civilization. London: Thames & Hudson, 2004. Accessed 09.04.2013.

Gillespie, Susan D. The Aztec Kings: The Construction of Rulership in Mexica History. Tucson: University of Arizona Press, 1989.

Gonzalez-Lauck, Rebecca. Venta, La (Tabasco, Mexico). Susan Toby Evans and David L. Webster (eds.). In Archaeology of Ancient Mexico and Central America: An Encyclopedia. New York: Garland Publications, 2001.

Gruzinski, Serge. The Aztecs: Rise and Fall of an Empire. New York: Harry N. Abrams, Inc., Publishers, 1992.

Hamnett, Brian. A Concise History of Mexico. UK: Cambridge University Press, 1999.

Killion, Thomas W., and Javier Urcid. The Olmec Legacy: Cultural Continuity and Change in Mexico's South Gulf Coast Lowlands. Accessed via: http://www.latinamericanstudies.org/totonac/olmec-legacy.pdf 09.03.2012.

(The) Pascua Yaqui Tribe of Arizona website: http://www.pascuayaquinsn.gov/index.php?option=com_content&view=article&id=28&Itemid=14. Accessed 08.26.2013.

(The) Pascua Yaqui Tribe of Arizona website: http://itcaonline.com/?page_id=1168. Accessed 08.29.2013.

Sabloff, Jeremy A. The Cities of Ancient Mexico: Reconstructing a Lost World. New York: Thames and Hudson, Inc., 1989.

Sahagun, Fray Bernardino de. Florentine Codex. Accessed via: http://books.google.com/books/about/Florentine_Codex.html?id=YflnAQAAMAAJ 09.11.2013.

Smith, Michael E., and Lisa Montiel. The Archaeological Study of Empires and Imperialism in Pre-Hispanic Central Mexico. Accessed via: http://www.public.asu.edu/~mesmith9/1-CompleteSet/MES-01-LM-Empires.pdf 08.28.2013.

Free Books by Charles River Editors

We have brand new titles available for free most days of the week. To see which of our titles are currently free, click on this link.

Discounted Books by Charles River Editors

We have titles at a discount price of just 99 cents everyday. To see which of our titles are currently 99 cents, click on this link.

Printed by Amazon Italia Logistica S.r.l.
Torrazza Piemonte (TO), Italy

52458642R00047